Monmouth Courthouse 1778

The last great battle in the North

Campaign • 135

OSPREY
PUBLISHING

Monmouth Courthouse 1778

The last great battle in the North

Brendan Morrissey • Illustrated by Adam Hook

Series editor Lee Johnson • Consultant editor David G Chandler

First published in Great Britain in 2004 by Osprey Publishing,
Midland House, West Way, Botley, Oxford OX2 0PH, UK
443 Park Avenue South, New York, NY 10016, USA
Email: info@ospreypublishing.com

A CIP catalogue record for this book is available from the British Library

ISBN 1 84176 772 7

Editor: Lee Johnson
Design: The Black Spot
Index by Alison Worthington
Maps by The Map Studio
3D bird's-eye views by The Black Spot
Battlescene artwork by Adam Hook
Originated by The Electronic Page Company, Cwmbran, UK
Printed in China through World Print Ltd.

05 06 07 08 09 10 9 8 7 6 5 4 3 2

For a catalog of all books published by Osprey Military
and Aviation please contact:

NORTH AMERICA
Osprey Direct, 2427 Bond Street, University Park, IL 60466, USA
E-mail: info@ospreydirectusa.com

ALL OTHER REGIONS
Osprey Direct UK, P.O. Box 140, Wellingborough,
Northants, NN8 2FA, UK
E-mail: info@ospreydirect.co.uk

www.ospreypublishing.com

Dedication

To Patrick and Emmet, and to Nora for the gift of them.

Acknowledgments

The author wishes to thank the following without whose
help this book would never have been completed: Dr Garry
Stone, curator of Monmouth Battlefield State Park, for
the enormous time and effort he put into reading and
correcting the text and orders of battle, and for generously
providing his own series of maps of the battle, upon which
the bird's-eye views have been based. Donald and Patricia
Post for their unstinting hospitality, and their son Todd for
his invaluable assistance and companionship in following
the routes taken by the two armies and in walking the
battlefield (especially that hedgerow).

Author's Note

For the sake of brevity and continuity, the author has
retained the terminology used in his earlier titles, *Boston
1775*, *Quebec 1775*, *Saratoga 1777* and *Yorktown 1781*
(Campaign Series Nos. 37, 128, 67 and 47): "American"
refers to the forces of Congress, and "Loyalist" to those
fighting for the King. The "native" peoples of North America
are referred to by their tribal names, or collectively as
"Indians" and retrospective terms such as "Native
American" and "Patriot" have been avoided. "New York"
refers to the colony/state and "New York City" to the
conurbation on the Manhattan peninsula.

Artist's note

Readers may care to note that the original paintings from
which the color plates in this book were prepared are
available for private sale. All reproduction copyright
whatsoever is retained by the Publishers. All enquiries
should be addressed to:

Scorpio Gallery
PO Box 475,
Hailsham,
East Sussex
BN27 2SL
UK

The Publishers regret that they can enter into no
correspondence upon this matter.

KEY TO MILITARY SYMBOLS

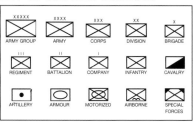

CONTENTS

THE ROAD TO MONMOUTH   7
Introduction • The seat of war

CHRONOLOGY   13

OPPOSING COMMANDERS   15
The British • The Americans

OPPOSING FORCES   19
The British and their allies • The Americans

THE MONMOUTH CAMPAIGN   26
Enter the French • Two roads to Monmouth • Washington's response
Monmouth Courthouse – The morning action • The afternoon action

AFTERMATH   75
Clinton reaches safety • Howe against D'Estaing
Lee's court-martial • Conclusion

ORDERS OF BATTLE   82
The Royal Army • The Continental Army

THE BATTLEFIELDS TODAY   91

FURTHER READING   94

INDEX   95

NORTH AMERICA, JANUARY 1778

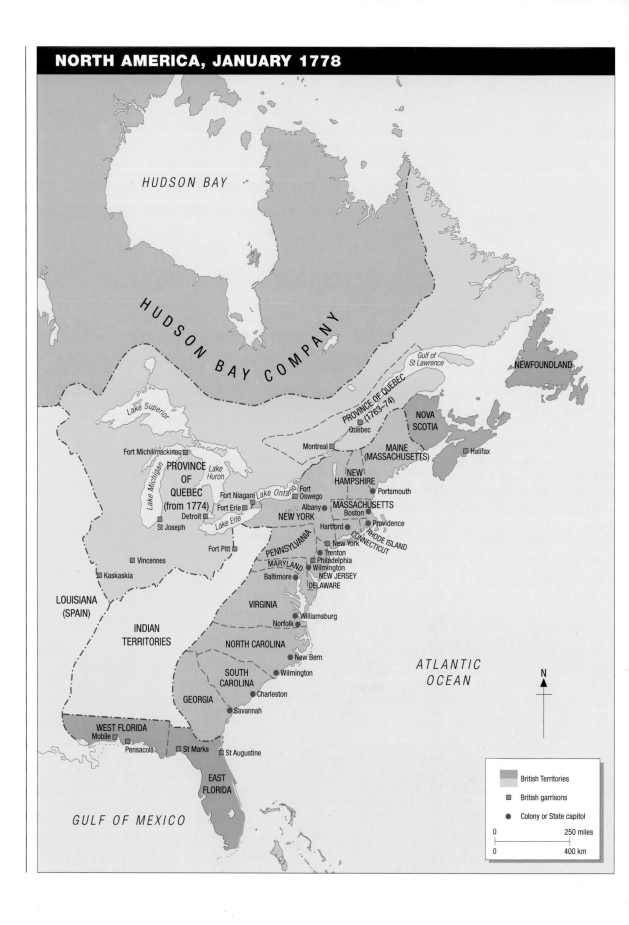

HUDSON BAY

HUDSON BAY COMPANY

Lake Superior

NEWFOUNDLAND

Gulf of
St Lawrence

PROVINCE OF QUEBEC
(1763–74)

NOVA
SCOTIA

Québec

Montreal

MAINE
(MASSACHUSETTS)

Halifax

Fort Michilimackinac

PROVINCE
OF
QUEBEC
(from 1774)

Lake Michigan

Lake
Huron

NEW
HAMPSHIRE

Portsmouth

Fort Niagara

Lake Ontario

Fort
Oswego

MASSACHUSETTS

Fort Erie

Albany

Boston

Detroit

Lake Erie

NEW YORK

Hartford

Providence

St Joseph

RHODE ISLAND

Fort Pitt

CONNECTICUT

Vincennes

PENNSYLVANIA

New York

Trenton

Kaskaskia

MARYLAND

Philadelphia

Wilmington

NEW JERSEY

LOUISIANA
(SPAIN)

Baltimore

DELAWARE

INDIAN
TERRITORIES

VIRGINIA

Williamsburg

Norfolk

NORTH CAROLINA

ATLANTIC
OCEAN

New Bern

N

SOUTH
CAROLINA

Wilmington

GEORGIA

Charleston

Savannah

WEST FLORIDA

Mobile

Pensacola

St Marks

St Augustine

EAST
FLORIDA

GULF OF MEXICO

British Territories

British garrisons

Colony or State capitol

0   250 miles

0   400 km

THE ROAD TO MONMOUTH

INTRODUCTION

Monmouth Courthouse was, according to many participants, the hardest fought engagement of the American Revolution. It was certainly the longest and, apart from the 1781 raid on Springfield, it was the last important action in the North. It was a "pell-mell" battle fought by regiments and detachments rather than brigades and divisions, and even today it is difficult to be certain of the exact sequence and timing of events. To these errors must be added the intensely partisan nature of opinions on the relationships between the two senior generals on each side, and the outcome of the battle itself.

The war in North America to December 1777

Following the outbreak of hostilities at Lexington and Concord on 19 April 1775, over 3,000 British troops were trapped in Boston by 20,000 New England militia. This situation was confirmed by the capture of Ticonderoga and Crown Point, and the battle of Bunker Hill – the first major action of the war. For the remainder of 1775, manpower shortages and a 3,000-mile supply line prevented any British breakout and gave General George Washington a chance to organize and train the new "Continental" army. Farther north, 2,000 men under Richard Montgomery and Benedict Arnold had captured St Johns and Montreal, and were besieging Quebec. Only a desperate defense of that city by Governor Guy Carleton prevented the loss of Canada, and the war.

Washington replaces Lee. A modern depiction of Continental infantrymen in action. The troops are in shirtsleeves, or wearing light linen hunting shirts and probably represent an accurate view of how Washington's men looked on those hot days in June 1778. (Mars, Lincolnshire)

Through the winter of 1775, Lord George Germain, the new Secretary of State for the American Colonies, organized and dispatched an imposing armada of almost 100 warships and hundreds of transports, carrying 13,000 sailors and 32,000 soldiers. It was led by Rear Admiral Lord Richard Howe and his younger brother, Lieutenant-General Sir William Howe, both favorites of King George III. However, a secondary expedition, a combined naval and land assault on Charleston, was repulsed, further demoralizing the Loyalists. More encouraging was the news from Canada, where Carleton had all but expelled the "Separate Army" and was preparing to recapture the Lake Champlain forts.

By August, the Howes had concentrated their forces off Staten Island, ready to capture New York City and cut off New England – still considered the seat of rebellion. Ordered by Congress to defend New York City, Washington suffered a series of defeats at the hands of Sir William Howe's forces. The latter proved unwilling (or unable) to follow up his initial successes, and a peace conference on Staten Island in September came to nothing.

Nevertheless, by December the British had captured New York City, the two forts guarding the lower Hudson River, and Newport, Rhode Island. Washington had no option but to retreat across New Jersey into Pennsylvania. Desperate for a victory to boost morale, he overwhelmed isolated outposts at Trenton and Princeton. Small as they were, these successes had enormous impact in Europe, where the Americans had been given no chance whatsoever of winning before.

The Howe brothers next decided to capture Philadelphia, the home of Congress. However, they ignored – or more likely were not fully aware of – a plan concocted by Burgoyne and Germain to isolate New England by simultaneous thrusts from Canada and New York City.

That summer, Sir William Howe landed on the Chesapeake Bay and inflicted yet another inconclusive defeat on Washington at Brandywine, then tricked him into leaving Philadelphia unguarded. In October, Washington attacked the British camp at Germantown, but an over-ambitious plan and poor generalship led to defeat. After a half-hearted pursuit, the British withdrew to Philadelphia for the winter, whilst Washington fell back 20 miles to Valley Forge.

Meanwhile, Burgoyne's expedition had begun well enough, with a practically bloodless recapture of Ticonderoga, but he then became bogged down in the wilderness of Upper New York. An ill-conceived foraging expedition cost him 10 percent of his army at Bennington, whilst farther west, a smaller expedition down the Mohawk Valley was halted at Fort Stanwix, and forced to retreat to Canada. Now completely

Lieutenant-General Sir Henry Clinton. His inability to work with, or control, subordinates was the result of a personality that fluctuated between over-assertiveness and excessive sensitivity. Unlike Howe, he was not popular with the British troops, but was liked by the German contingents, as he spoke fluent German. (National Army Museum)

East view of Philadelphia. Prior to its occupation, Philadelphia was the second largest city in the British Empire (after London), with 35,000 inhabitants. Unfortunately, its location made it easy to blockade, especially for French ships from the Caribbean. (Private collection)

isolated and facing a numerically superior enemy, Burgoyne fought two indecisive encounters at Freeman's Farm and Bemis Heights, then procrastinated for several days until left with no option but to surrender with his remaining 5,000 men at Saratoga.

If Trenton and Princeton had surprised Europe, Saratoga inspired some of its rulers to reconsider their policy toward America. France, in particular, saw an opportunity to avenge the humiliating peace of 1763, and began turning covert aid into active military involvement. A colonial rebellion was about to become a world war.

THE SEAT OF WAR

The most fought-over of the Thirteen Colonies, New Jersey – later called the cockpit of the Revolution – did not see a shot fired in anger until June 1776, but from that November onward suffered six years of bitter conflict. The British occupation of New York City generated constant raids and foraging expeditions, and even when conventional forces departed, Loyalist and Rebel militias, bands of escaped slaves, and common high-waymen prevented any respite.

Geography and history
At 150 miles (242km) long and 70 miles (113km) wide, New Jersey was the fourth smallest of the Thirteen Colonies, occupying 8,700 square miles (1,200 of them covered by water) between the Hudson River and the Atlantic in the east, and the Delaware River in the west. There were three distinct geographic regions, known today as the Atlantic Coastal Plain; the Piedmont, containing the Hudson, Passaic, Remapo, and Raritan Rivers; and the New England Upland (known in the 18th century as The Highlands) extending northward into Pennsylvania and New York. The Atlantic Coastal Plain covered 5,000 square miles, including lowland areas (mostly less than 100 feet (30m) above sea level) between Philadelphia and Sandy Hook, with gently rolling hills, pine barrens, and the occasional salt marsh.

The climate included hot, humid summers and cold winters, with average temperatures ranging from 85° to 25° Fahrenheit (29.4° to minus 4° centigrade), although they could fall below minus 30° and exceed 100° and often did in the 1770s. Charles Lee remarked that summers in New York and New Jersey could be as hot as any in Spain, and many observers noted the sandy roads were difficult to march on. Rainfall was plentiful (typically up to 48 inches annually) and summer storms were often heavy and thundery.

Overall, the weather and the sandy, fertile soil made the area ideal for farming, in turn creating a predominantly rural society, with few large conurbations and a landscape dotted with orchards and fields, producing mainly cereals, flax, hemp, and cranberries. The only manufacturing industry consisted of some iron foundries in the south and west, and a glass-blowing house near Salem.

Politics and people
Originally populated by Algonquins, the area had been settled by Swedes and Dutch in the mid-17th century, before coming under English control

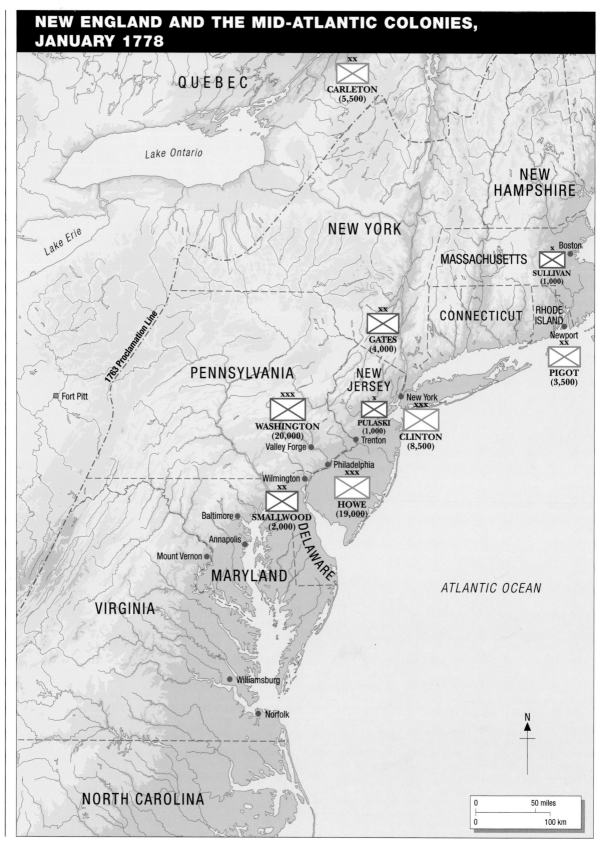

Brigadier-General Sir William Erskine (1728–95) by Sir Joshua Reynolds. Erskine was a cavalry officer who had fought at Emsdorf in 1762, and commanded a brigade at Long Island. As Clinton's Quartermaster General, he was responsible not only for supply, but also for troop movements, reconnaissance, encampments and transportation. (National Portrait Gallery)

after 1674. Two years later, it was divided into East and West Jersey and although Quakers progressively settled both, an east–west division persisted until the war, with the colony still often referred to as "the Jerseys". Apart from a brief spell as part of New England, the Jerseys were self-governing until 1702, from when they were administered by the governor of New York, but with their own assembly. In 1738, the first royal governor of an independent New Jersey was appointed, but the next two decades saw land riots and other unrest caused by long-standing disputes over proprietary titles. Another problem – the boundary with New York – was only settled by a Royal Commission in 1774.

By the 1770s, a distinct social and religious *milieu* had evolved. Most large estates lay in East Jersey, but the colony as a whole was mainly middle-class and rural. Quakers were the majority in the west, Presbyterians in the central region, and Anglicans in the east – divisions that matched almost exactly the distribution of neutral, pro- and anti-revolution groups respectively. The loyalties of these sects matched their counterparts in other colonies. Bergen and Monmouth counties were Tory, whilst the south and the mainly Presbyterian Essex and Middlesex counties were Whig.

In 1775, the population numbered around 130,000, of whom almost 10,000 were black, virtually all of them slaves whose importance to the labor market was reflected in some of the harshest slavery laws in North America. Of the 120,000 whites, over half were English; another 20,000 were Ulster Irish, a similar number were Dutch, 12,000 were Germans, and the remainder were French Huguenots and Swedes. There were 110 men for every 100 women and only 40 percent of the population lived south of the Raritan River.

New Jersey was moderate in its relations with Great Britain. A small merchant class and predominantly rural economy was affected little by import and export controls, and there were no newspapers to inflame opinion. A large, passive Quaker community, and a Royal Governor,

The baggage train. The British evacuation of Philadelphia required over 1,500 wagons, stretching between eight and 12 miles, according to various accounts. That not one vehicle was lost en route to Sandy Hook says much for the degree of protection afforded by the various units detailed to guard it. (Private collection)

The approach to Monmouth Courthouse. This view, made in 1850, still shows the undulating nature of the countryside that caused Major General Charles Lee so many problems because of his failure to reconnoiter. (Private collection)

William Franklin (son of Benjamin), avoided conflict by focusing attention on local needs. Other than objecting to the Quartering Act in 1771, New Jersey took little part in the pre-war bickering with Parliament and was one of the last colonies to support independence. Its constitution, drafted in July 1776, even had a "voiding" clause should a political solution be found.

The catalyst for New Jersey's involvement in the war was Washington's flight from New York, but the resulting social rifts still owed more to traditional ethnic, socio-economic, and religious differences than to clashes of political philosophy. The situation was further complicated by farmers living close to areas under British control, who came to value hard cash above principles. In 1776, Franklin was imprisoned in Connecticut and replaced by the moderate Whig, William Livingston, who tried to rein in the more extreme elements of the Rebel community (avoiding demands to fine Quakers for their neutrality for example). Despite this, attitudes and behavior on both sides hardened noticeably as the war went on.

Militarily, New Jersey was most active during the first two years of the war. It raised four line infantry regiments for Continental service, reduced to three after 1778, and two from 1781, due to lack of recruits. It also raised two Additional regiments, both disbanded in 1779, again due to lack of recruits. Two artillery companies were raised as State troops in 1776, but later absorbed into the Continental Army. In 1776, New Jersey had 1,700 Continentals in Canada and 2,000 militia at New York City; by 1777, there were 1,200 Continentals and 1,000 militia with Washington in Pennsylvania. In June 1778, the four regiments still had 1,200 men, supported by 1,000 militia called out for 30 days' service (replacing a similar number discharged at the end of May). By contrast, New Jersey Loyalists filled three eponymous regiments, the largest initially having six battalions numbering 2,500 men, and swelled the ranks of many more units raised in New York City and Philadelphia. Throughout the war New Jersey may have emulated New York in producing more full-time soldiers for the King than for Congress.

CHRONOLOGY

1775

19 April Skirmishes at Lexington and Concord
15 May New Jersey Provincial Congress replaces Royal Assembly
15 June Washington becomes Continental commander in chief
9 October First New Jersey regiments authorized by Continental Congress
16 October British transport *Rebecca & Francis* burned on Brigantine Beach
(first ship lost on either side in New Jersey waters)

1776

6 February New Jersey's Royal Governor, William Franklin, arrested
29 June Skirmish at Cape May: first casualty on New Jersey soil
2 July New Jersey Provincial Congress adopts new constitution
2–4 July Continental Congress declares the Thirteen Colonies independent
18 July Provincial Congress becomes Convention of the state of New Jersey
22 August–20 November New York campaign
31 August William Livingston elected Governor of New Jersey
11 September Peace conference on Staten Island
20 November Fort Lee abandoned to the British
21 November–25 December Washington's retreat through New Jersey
11 December Pennsylvania Navy bombards Burlington
13 December Lee captured at Basking Ridge
26 December Battle of Trenton

1777

2–3 January Actions at Assunpink Creek and Princeton
6 January–28 May Continental Army in winter quarters at Morristown
12–30 June British fail to trap Washington around New Brunswick
27 July La Fayette arrives in Philadelphia
25 August–20 November Philadelphia campaign
19 December Continental Army arrives at Valley Forge

1778

2 January Washington exposes "Conway Cabal" to Congress
22 January–18 March Congress plans second invasion of Canada
6 February France signs treaty of alliance
23 February Von Steuben arrives at Valley Forge
2 March Wayne and Pulaski attack Simcoe at Cooper's Ferry
11 March North's Conciliatory Acts given Royal Assent
13 March France declares war on Great Britain
18–21 March Actions at Quinton's Bridge and Hancock's Bridge
23 April Lee arrives at Valley Forge following exchange
1 May Action at Crooked Billet
3–8 May British fortify Cooper's Ferry
7–10 May British raid on Bordentown
8 May Clinton arrives in Philadelphia
18 May Sir William Howe's *Meschianza*
20 May Action at Barren Hill

24 May Clinton replaces Sir William Howe as commander in chief
25 May Sir William Howe returns to England
6 June Carlisle Peace Commission arrives in Philadelphia
June–November Peace Commission fails in attempts to negotiate with Congress

THE CAMPAIGN

15–17 June British cross the Delaware at Cooper's Ferry
18 June Lord Howe sails for New York, Clinton reaches Haddonfield. Lee and Wayne cross the Schuykill
19 June Clinton reaches Evesham. Washington marches to Doylestown, Arnold arrives in Philadelphia
20 June Clinton reaches Mount Holly. Lee and Wayne cross the Delaware, Washington reaches Buckingham
21 June Clinton remains at Mount Holly, joined by Knyphausen and baggage train. Washington crosses the Delaware
22 June Clinton marches to Black Horse (now Columbus)
23 June Skirmish at Crosswicks; Clinton marches to Allentown. Washington reaches Hopewell, detachment sent to join Morgan
24 June Council-of-war: Scott sent to harass Clinton. Cornwallis reaches Allentown; Knyphausen reaches Imlaystown
25 June Clinton opts to march to Sandy Hook; reverses order of march. Washington marches to Rocky Hill, La Fayette and Wayne join Scott
26 June Clinton marches to Monmouth Courthouse. Washington arrives at Cranberry, La Fayette reaches Englishtown
27 June Clinton remains at Monmouth Courthouse. Council of war: Lee takes over command from La Fayette

28 JUNE 1778

4.00am Knyphausen leaves Monmouth Courthouse
6.00am Grayson's detachment leaves Englishtown
7.30am Dickinson's militia skirmishes with Queen's Rangers
8.00am Rest of Lee's division leaves Englishtown
9.00am Lee's division resumes march after halt at Tennent Meetinghouse
9.30am Butler and Jackson skirmish with British outposts near Monmouth Courthouse
10.00am British cavalry attack Butler's detachment
10.30am La Fayette extends Lee's right
11.00am Cornwallis returns, Scott and Maxwell attempt to form new line
11.30am La Fayette forced to fall back, retreat becomes general
12.00pm Lee meets Washington
12.30pm Stewart and Ramsay attack Foot Guards; Greene moves to Craig's Mills
1.00pm Defence of hedgerow and pursuit across West Morass
1.30pm Artillery duel begins
2.00pm Erskine outflanks Washington's left and is opposed by La Fayette
2.30pm Steuben re-forms Lee's division at Englishtown
3.00pm Erskine withdraws to Craig Farm, Comb's Hill battery opens fire
3.30pm Clinton orders withdrawal
4.00pm Fighting in Sutfin Orchard
5.00pm Wayne's attack and fighting at Parsonage Farm
6.00pm Clinton falls back towards Monmouth Courthouse; Poor follows
10.00pm Clinton resumes march to Sandy Hook

AFTERMATH

29 June Clinton's army reaches Middletown. Howe's fleet leaves Delaware Bay
30 June Clinton and Howe arrive at Sandy Hook. Washington leaves Englishtown
1–5 July Clinton's army evacuated to New York City
1–24 July Washington marches from Brunswick to White Plains
4 July–12 August Court-martial of Lee at New Brunswick
5–11 July Howe prepares to defend New York harbour
11–23 July D'Estaing's fleet at Sandy Hook
23 October–5 December Congress reviews Lee's court-martial
27 November Carlisle Commission returns to England

OPPOSING COMMANDERS

Lieutenant-General Charles, Earl Cornwallis. Brave and energetic on the battlefield, Cornwallis was known to be a favorite of Lord George Germain (which Clinton was not) and this, along with his "dormant commission", led to distrust between the two men. (National Portrait Gallery, London)

THE BRITISH

Lieutenant-General Sir Henry Clinton (1738–95) was the only son of a former governor of New York, and served as a militia officer before moving to England. He joined the Foot Guards in 1751, serving in Germany from 1760 to 1762 as a regimental officer and, later, *aide* to Ferdinand of Brunswick. Family connections helped him become an MP and after being promoted to major-general in 1772, he was one of the three generals sent to Boston three years later. For his bravery leading the final assault at Bunker Hill, he received the local rank of lieutenant-general and became second-in-command to Sir William Howe. Unfortunately, they did not get on; Clinton was always offering unwanted advice and Howe constantly sought opportunities to move him elsewhere, such as the Carolinas or Rhode Island.

Blamed publicly by Germain for the Charleston fiasco, Clinton came back to England at the end of 1776 planning to resign, but was placated by a promotion and a knighthood. He returned to America in July 1777, but found that Howe had not begun his campaign, whilst Burgoyne (nominally Clinton's subordinate) was leading the Canadian army. Though trapped in New York City by larger forces, Clinton still managed a well-organized raid into the Hudson Highlands in a vain attempt to rescue Burgoyne. However, when he finally replaced Howe as commander in chief, he found himself stuck with a new strategy that he opposed and insufficient resources to carry it out.

Upset by Cornwallis's "dormant commission" and insubordinate actions in the South (which he felt Germain had encouraged), Clinton submitted another resignation, which was accepted. He returned to England in 1782 to find himself the scapegoat for Yorktown, and two years later was ousted from Parliament. He regained his seat in 1790, was made a general in 1783, and became Governor of Gibraltar in 1794, but died a year later.

Clinton had few opportunities to shine as a battlefield leader; he was less inspiring than Burgoyne or Howe, and not as audacious as Cornwallis. However, his strategic vision and planning skills were probably unrivalled by any other Royal commander. He understood that large-scale Loyalist support required a permanent military presence, and his family links with the Royal Navy helped him to appreciate the dependence of his army on sea power. His main shortcomings – caution and insecurity – were inflamed by the dispatch of half his army to the Caribbean and the return of the only capable naval commander he had – Lord Howe – to Europe. He inevitably fell out with subordinates or equals before very long, and bombarded superiors with bold plans for which they, rather than he, would be ultimately responsible. His egotism was of the self-pitying, rather than self-confident, variety that often marks out the great commander.

Lieutenant-General Charles, Earl Cornwallis (1738–1805), was educated at Eton and a military academy in Turin, and joined the 1st Foot Guards as a teenager. He saw considerable service in Europe, during the Seven Years War, until the death of his father led him into the House of Lords as the second Earl Cornwallis. Although a Whig, he held several Court and staff posts during the 1760s, before becoming a major-general in 1775. Despite opposing the policies that had caused the rebellion, he agreed to serve in America, and was chosen to be Carleton's second-in-command in Canada, but was replaced by Burgoyne.

He left Cork with 2,500 men in February 1776, to join Clinton off Cape Fear and, after the unsuccessful attack on Charleston, played important roles at Long Island, Kip's Bay, and Fort Washington. However, he failed to fulfill his boast of "bagging the fox" in New Jersey, and Washington's escape and subsequent victories led to considerable criticism from Clinton and others.

After wintering in England, Cornwallis returned to command a division in the Philadelphia campaign (of which he was one of the few advocates), and fought at Brandywine and Germantown. In January 1778, he was promoted to lieutenant-general and became Clinton's second-in-command, with a "dormant commission" to succeed him. Inevitably, Clinton saw a conspiracy, but in fact this was to ensure that command devolved to a British officer, as the senior Hessian officer, von Knyphausen, was technically senior to Cornwallis. During the march across New Jersey, Cornwallis commanded the rearguard and personally led the counterattack against Lee's division on 28 June, for which "zealous service" he was commended in Clinton's report. He spent that winter in England with his dying wife, and did not return to America until July 1779.

At the start of 1780 Clinton began to confide in him, expecting to have his latest resignation accepted. When it was not, relations between them soured and it was a relief when Clinton returned to New York City, leaving Cornwallis in charge in the South. Unfortunately, Cornwallis's strategic view was much more aggressive than Clinton's and, having sought and obtained authority from Germain to operate semi-independently, the former began the campaign that ended at Yorktown.

Exchanged in May 1782, Cornwallis returned to England a hero, despite constant arguments with Clinton over the conduct of the war. In 1786, he went to India and built a reputation as a general and administrator. He became the 1st Marquis Cornwallis in 1793, returned to England in 1794, and was briefly governor general and commander in chief in Ireland. He returned to India in 1805, but died soon after arriving.

His military personality changed during the war, most notably after the death of his wife. In particular, he was far stricter about plundering and other acts of indiscipline – by officers or men – prior to 1779. Frustrated personal ambitions, and occasional operational setbacks, led to inconsistency in his behavior, both on and off the battlefield. His background led him to believe that he should have greater responsibility in America, but that view was not shared: one of Clinton's *aides* called him "insipid [and] good natured" but "the worst officer (but in personal courage) under the Crown."

Lieutenant-General Wilhelm Freiherr von Knyphausen (1716–1800). Knyphausen joined the Prussian army in 1734 and by 1775 was a lieutenant general in Hesse-Kassel service. Arriving in America in October 1776, he led the attack on Fort Washington (later renamed in his honor), and commanded a division in the Philadelphia campaign. In June 1778, he saw little fighting, but did protect Clinton's massive baggage train on the last stages of its journey to Sandy Hook. From 1777, he commanded all the Hessian troops in America, but was also briefly de facto second-in-command of all Royal forces on the continent – hence Cornwallis's "dormant commission". After the Springfield raid in May 1781, ill-health forced him to return home. Despite the famous cartoon of him buttering bread with his thumb, he was a slim, well-mannered officer, who was popular with his men. Though never treated as an equal by his allies, he proved capable and reliable. (Private collection)

Major General Charles Lee (1732–82) by an unknown artist. Nicknamed "Ounewaterika" (boiling water) by the Mohawks because of his fiery temper, Lee was as egotistical and vain as Washington was reserved and modest. Yet despite his appalling manners and a critical outlook, Lee was noted for his witty conversation and observers on both sides considered him a more capable general than Washington. (Private collection)

Cornwallis craved action, and had his wish in the early years, but gradually became disillusioned with the war and Clinton's passive strategy, and had requested a recall on the day the British left Philadelphia. Despite his own reputation for aggressiveness, he agreed with criticism of Clinton leading charges like a "Newmarket jockey" at Monmouth, but their post-war clashes tend to overshadow the fact that their personal relationship in 1778 was, if not friendly, at least civil and cordial. In England, Cornwallis visited Clinton's motherless children, whilst Clinton was happy to entrust him with urgent requests for troops, and to commend Cornwallis's knowledge of America to ministers. The successful evacuation of Philadelphia and the rearguard action at Monmouth illustrated what could be done with Clinton in charge of strategy and Cornwallis handling tactics.

THE AMERICANS

Major General Charles Lee (1731–82) was born in England and attended a military school in Switzerland before joining the Army in 1744. In 1754, he went to America with his father's regiment, the 44th Foot, fought at Monongahela, and was posted to New York, where he was adopted by Mohawks and married a chief's daughter. He was wounded at Ticonderoga in 1758, and attended the capture of Niagara and Montreal, before returning to England. In 1762, he served in Portugal under Burgoyne, then retired briefly on half-pay before joining the Polish Army as an *aide* to King Stanislaus. He reached the rank of major general and then fought for the Russians against the Turks, before touring Europe and losing two fingers in a duel in Italy. He was promoted to lieutenant-colonel in British service in 1772, but with no active posts available, he resigned his commission.

A committed Whig, Lee had long been interested in the dispute with Parliament and in 1773, emigrated to America, settling in Virginia. In 1775, he immediately offered his services to Congress, believing that his experience might see him appointed commander in chief. He was not surprised to lose out to the native-born Washington but was outraged when Artemas Ward was made second-in-command and criticized the appointment (although Ward's ill-health meant Lee was *de facto* second-in-command outside New England).

After serving at Boston, Lee supervised the construction of the defenses of New York City, before taking command of the Southern Department in March 1776. In June, he arrived in Charleston to organize the defenses there, and during the British attack advised Moultrie to abandon Fort Sullivan. Recalled to New York City, he fought at White Plains and took on an independent command at Peekskill, where his delay in rejoining Washington led to speculation about his loyalty to his superior. In December 1776, Lee was captured at White's Tavern in Basking Ridge and was going to be tried as a deserter – and thus liable to hang – until Congress confirmed that he had resigned his British commission before accepting theirs. As Congress did not hold any high-ranking British officers, Lee was not exchanged until May 1778, after a British general had been kidnapped specifically for that purpose.

Of all the former British officers in Continental service, Lee was considered the most talented – by both sides. In March 1777, he apparently sent Howe a plan to win the war by seizing Annapolis, Alexandria, and Baltimore, thereby isolating the South. Whilst the document is *prima facie* treasonable, Lee favored a negotiated peace and may have felt that, with an American victory unlikely, this was the best way to end the war quickly. (Given his intellectual vanity it is not inconceivable that it was merely a theoretical exercise generated by conversations with Clinton and others, whilst in captivity.)

The military and political career of **General George Washington** (1732–99) is well known, and it is probably more valuable to consider his relationship with Lee during the summer of 1778, and other issues that may have been on his mind at that time. He began the year struggling with Congress over the supply of essentials to his troops, whose sufferings at Valley Forge clearly touched him. He also had to deal with the Conway Cabal, criticism from Congress of his defense of Philadelphia the previous year, and the re-publication of forged letters supposedly illustrating his "real" views on the war. Increasingly, his record of failure in major battles was contrasted with the victory at Saratoga, with Gates being openly touted as an alternative commander in chief.

General George Washington (1732–99) by C.W. Peale. Washington was every inch the commander – tall, well-mannered, composed, brave, and dignified. However, the Conway Cabal, the forged letters, and the critical comparisons with Gates, must – at least in part – have influenced his desire to bring Clinton to battle. (Independence National Historical Park)

Another problem was Washington's relationship with Lee, whose apparently superior intellect and military record (though certainly not his personal habits) may have caused some awkwardness. Their respective educations bore no comparison – Washington's ended at 15, leaving him deficient in most subjects except mathematics, not well read, and a poor public speaker. Like many, he was impressed at first by Lee's ability to speak several languages, and the fact that he had fought in battles on two continents and touched the hands of kings.

However, by 1778, Washington also knew Lee's opinion of him, having accidentally opened a letter in which Lee referred to a "… fatal indecision of mind which in war is a much greater disqualification than stupidity or even want of personal courage." It speaks highly of Washington that, when Lee first came to Valley Forge after his exchange, Washington had the entire army parade along the route, and rode out four miles to meet him. (Typically, Lee expressed his gratitude by promptly riding off to lobby Congress for a role in possible peace negotiations.) By the time of the British evacuation of Philadelphia, the relationship must have cooled. When Lee wrote to Washington advising him against continuously moving officers from one division to another, Washington replied that he and other generals were all sufficiently well acquainted with each other for it not to matter, but also remarked somewhat testily to the amount of "advice" Lee was presuming to give.

Prior to the Monmouth campaign, Washington's own morale must have been at a low ebb. Whilst he was no doubt gratified at how his field commanders – Greene, Stirling, Wayne, and the ever-faithful La Fayette – rallied round him, he was clearly stung by the constant criticism and admitted as much to Patrick Henry. There is little doubt that he was under pressure to win a major battle, which only added to his existing burdens as commander in chief. It explains (at least in part) his eagerness to bring on a full-scale engagement with Clinton, despite the advice of his experienced foreign officers, including Steuben, Du Portail, and, of course, Lee.

OPPOSING FORCES

THE BRITISH AND THEIR ALLIES

Major General the Marquis de La Fayette (1757–1834) by C.W. Peale. La Fayette was only 19, spoke no English, and had no military experience when he arrived in America. The haughtiness and false credentials of previous arrivals guaranteed a chilly reception and initially, he had to serve as a volunteer at his own expense (to his credit, he was one of the very few foreigners who served primarily out of idealism). Distinguished service at Brandywine and strong support for Washington led to him being given command of a brigade in 1777. He provided a valuable link with other French officers in America and was chosen (albeit as a figurehead) to lead the planned invasion of Canada. Though well liked, he remained inexperienced and hot-headed and his selection to lead the Barren Hill operation was widely criticized. (Independence National Historical Park)

Most of the British troops in Philadelphia in January 1778 were veterans of two, or even three, years' fighting, and whilst the harsh winter and the boredom of garrison life may have affected discipline, it had not diminished their self-confidence. The regimental officers enjoyed the confidence of the rank-and-file and, supported by experienced NCOs, provided effective battlefield leadership. However, these same qualities made them difficult to command; on taking over from Howe, Clinton wrote: "… every officer in the army was a general – and not only gave his opinions, but acted with an independence destructive of all order, subordination, and discipline …"

The British Regulars

Three quarters of the infantry served in the 20 "line" regiments, which were numbered in order of seniority, and had a nominal strength of 665 officers and men each, in ten companies. On paper, each company had three officers, three sergeants, two drummers, and 58 rank-and-file, but actual strength was invariably below this, more often through sickness rather than combat. Eight companies (known as "center companies" or "hatmen") formed the main body of the unit on campaign. The other two – one of grenadiers, one of light infantry – were detached from the unit and served alongside those of other regiments in "converged" battalions. In 1778, the grenadier and light battalions were large units – returns suggest 12 to 14 companies each – and were usually split into two "wings" in action.

The Foot Guards had their own structure, comprising two battalions, each of four center companies and a flank company – grenadiers in the 1st Battalion, light infantry in the 2nd Battalion (their flank companies were not detached, but often operated as distinct units because of their large size). Along with the flank battalions, the Foot Guards were the elite of the army, providing a highly motivated body of men who could be relied upon in the toughest situations. Whilst the flank battalions stripped the line units of their best men – both initially and in replacing losses – they enjoyed almost talismanic status within the army and Clinton was severely criticized when he disbanded them after Monmouth.

Though the terms were often interchangeable, regiments and companies were primarily administrative units; the principal tactical formations were the battalion and the platoon, the latter being the basic unit for firing and maneuvering. Throughout the Monmouth campaign, the British infantry fought in two-rank lines, in either close, open, or extended order (in practice, the first meant that adjacent men had their elbows touching, the second involved a gap of 18 inches between files, and

the last a space of up to five feet). Howe had abandoned the three-rank line for these looser, two-rank formations in 1776; Clinton disapproved but kept them as Washington had no cavalry capable of exploiting their weakness. Live firing and marksmanship were practiced frequently, and the grenadier and most "line" battalions were just as adept as the light infantry at moving and fighting in broken country.

The two cavalry units in Philadelphia, the 16th and 17th Light Dragoons, specialized in outpost work, reconnaissance, escort duty and acting as couriers. Personal responsibility and initiative were emphasized and the men were well treated, and hence saw themselves as an elite force. In 1776, both regiments had adopted a new establishment of six mounted and six dismounted troops, effectively becoming the type of legionary corps championed by Marshal de Saxe. Mounted troops usually had three officers, one sergeant, one musician and 39 rank-and-file, dismounted troops one cornet and 33 enlisted men. However, returns from May and July 1778 suggest both types of unit were considerably under strength. Regimental staff comprised a lieutenant-colonel, a major, a chaplain, an adjutant, and a surgeon, plus various craftsmen.

British light infantry (front & rear), by P.J. de Loutherbourg c.1778. Contrary to the popular image of the inflexible, outwitted redcoat, the British light infantry were a constant thorn in Washington's side. By 1778, their clothing adaptations and tactics had been introduced throughout the British infantry. (Anne S.K. Brown Collection)

The Royal Regiment of Artillery had 12 companies in Philadelphia, drawn mainly from the 1st Battalion. Each comprised a captain and six other officers, three sergeants, three corporals, 20 gunners, 62 matrosses (semi-skilled men who physically moved the guns in action) and two drummers. Average company strength was just over 50 men and the gunners had to be augmented by retrained Loyalist infantry. Guns and vehicles were allotted according to the company's current role. In the field, this was mainly a pair of 3-pdr or 6-pdr "battalion guns" attached to a brigade (or sometimes to an individual battalion) for direct fire support, or occasionally the heavier 12-pdr and $5\frac{1}{2}$in. howitzers of the army's artillery reserve.

The German troops

When war broke out, several German rulers had offered military aid to the King, but had been politely rebuffed. However, it soon became clear

OPPOSITE **British light dragoons skirmishing c.1775. The two Regular cavalry regiments with Clinton were well-trained, elite units, whose skill at the *petite guerre* protected his vulnerable baggage train during the campaign. However, difficult terrain and stubborn resistance made their attempts at the traditional battlefield charge less successful on 28 June.**

that there were insufficient British troops to subdue the colonists and six minor states were paid to supply contingents of varying sizes. Units from two contingents – Hesse-Kassel (true "Hessians") and Anspach-Bayreuth – were in Philadelphia.

The Hesse-Kassel forces comprised a grenadier brigade of three battalions, five single-battalion infantry regiments, a Jäger Korps (including a mounted troop), and an artillery company. Two infantry regiments were "fusiliers", which entailed slight uniform differences but otherwise had no real military significance; a third was an ad hoc unit formed to absorb the steady trickle of men captured at Trenton who had escaped American captivity. The jägers were among the best troops on either side, matching the accuracy and guile of Morgan's riflemen, but being generally superior in terms of discipline.

Hesse-Kassel units were unique in that they had to serve under their own generals – in this case Knyphausen. The regiments were trained, organized and equipped along Prussian lines, with a theoretical strength of 18 staff, and five companies, each of four officers, 13 NCOs, three drummers, and 105 rank-and-file. In 1776, Howe had encouraged all German infantry to adopt two-rank formations; most did, but retained "close" order, believing the "open" order used by the British was too weak.

The Anspach-Bayreuth contingent – two infantry regiments and a company each of jägers and gunners – only arrived in America in June 1777, and was apparently not highly regarded. Each regiment had one grenadier and four musketeer companies, all with a nominal strength of 112 officers and men, plus regimental staff and a detachment of artillerymen. Unusually, the grenadiers remained with the regiments, but the jägers were detached to the Jäger Korps.

The Loyalists

In the early years of the war, Government policy on the mobilization of Loyalists appeared confused. This is often ascribed to official arrogance, but from the start, many generals and politicians realized that using local forces could create rifts that would make post-war reconciliation more difficult. However, as the war progressed and bitterness evolved of its own accord, manpower became the more pressing issue and from 1776, units of "Provincials" were raised, trained, organized, and equipped similarly to the Regulars. The Provincials made up 10 percent of Clinton's army, with units ranging from 60 to 370 strong, including several troops of horse. Some of these units had been formed since the capture of Philadelphia and included deserters and "turned" prisoners of war; almost all were untried in combat. Consequently, they were used primarily for second-line duties, such as policing the city, manning the less exposed posts, and guarding the baggage train.

However, a few units raised in New York in 1776 had acquired good reputations, such as the New Jersey Volunteers, raised by Cortland Skinner (whose 2nd Battalion provided four companies of matrosses for the Royal Artillery), and the Guides and Pioneers who, despite their name, encompassed every branch of military service from scouts and spies to engineers and surveyors. Finally, the Queen's Rangers – under a British Regular officer, John Graves Simcoe – was evolving into the archetypal legion, or partisan corps. Originally raised by Robert Rogers, it was organized as an infantry battalion, but with an additional light company

(referred to as "Highlanders") and a troop of hussars. Such was its reputation that it was entrusted with outpost duties during the occupation of Philadelphia, and formed part of the rearguard during the march through New Jersey.

THE AMERICANS

In 1777, Congress had finally accepted the idea of a standing army, authorizing three-year enlistments and the establishment of permanent regiments. No longer required to disband his army and create a new one from scratch at the end of each year, Washington could now maintain a cadre of experienced, disciplined officers and men, and permanent, professional staffs. In addition, 1777 had seen two major tactical developments: the use of the brigade as the principal battlefield unit, and the creation of a corps of "light infantry" chosen from the best men in every regiment. The refinements introduced by Steuben – who regarded Americans as the finest raw material for an army he had ever encountered – completed the creation of a more robust, professional force, confirming the view of a Hessian jäger officer that the Continentals needed only "time and good leadership to make them formidable."

Infantry

For 1777, Congress had approved an army of 110 infantry, three artillery, four cavalry, and two "support" regiments, with a paper strength of just over 90,000. By early 1778, most of these units had been posted to Washington's Main Army, or else had transferred to it after the victory at Saratoga. Each of the artillery and cavalry regiments, and 88 of the infantry units, were assigned to a specific state, according to quotas based on population. The other 22 infantry regiments were unassigned, but recruited in one or two areas where their senior officers were well known.

In January 1778, the infantry were still using the "November 1775" organization, which included three field officers (colonel, lieutenant colonel and major) and ten staff, with eight companies, each of four officers, four sergeants, two musicians and 80 rank-and-file. In May 1778, a new structure reduced the numbers of officers and enlisted men to save money and to acknowledge the reality of poor recruitment, whilst a ninth "light" company was formed for detached service. However, most states did not introduce these changes until the end of 1778, and in some cases well into 1779, although there were light companies in the two North Carolina regiments, and extra rifle-armed companies in some Pennsylvania and Virginia regiments during the campaign.

Following the capable, if unspectacular, performance of the light infantry corps in 1777, the Monmouth campaign saw the formation of numerous ad hoc battalions of "picked men" from various regiments and brigades. It has been suggested that the presence of these units contributed, at least in part, to the poor performance of Lee's division on 28 June. It is arguable that homogenous, existing units might have had more cohesion and *esprit de corps*. However, the method of selection meant that the provisional units contained the best officers (some of whom had served in the 1777 corps) and men from Washington's army, whose experience would have been diluted within the established state line regiments, because of the large numbers of raw recruits and untried men that the latter contained. The best example of such a unit was the corps commanded by Morgan, which included Virginia and Pennsylvania rifle companies, supported by small groups of men from each infantry brigade, chosen for their marksmanship.

Cavalry

The mounted arm of Washington's army consisted of the four light dragoon regiments authorized by Congress in 1777. Towards the end of 1777, they had been brigaded for the first time, under the Polish volunteer Casimir Pulaski, to create an offensive force capable of shock action (though subsequent changes in strategic and tactical needs saw them revert to their previous roles, which were similar to their British counterparts). The brigade had wintered at Trenton, rather than Valley Forge, to ensure enough forage and to allow Pulaski time and space to train the men and horses. However, he resigned in March 1778 after disagreements with his American subordinates. Washington could not find a suitable replacement in time and this, along with a shortage of horses, kept the brigade out of the campaign. Only small detachments from the Continental regiments and a few mounted New Jersey militia served in June 1778.

Artillery

The Continental Artillery corps evolved from a few militia companies that had often become gunners merely on the whim of their captains. The experiences of 1775 and 1776 had shown the need for a more professional approach, and while state and other proprietorial interests still existed in 1778, four of the five regiments demanded by the commander of the corps, Henry Knox, had been established. The first, under Charles Harrison, comprised ten companies from Virginia, and later included the three large companies sent by Maryland to support its two infantry brigades. The second, commanded by John Lamb, had one "Continental" company, five from New York, and two each from Connecticut and Pennsylvania. The third, under John Crane, contained nine Massachusetts companies. The fourth, led by John Proctor, had ten Pennsylvania companies.

On paper, each company had five officers, six sergeants, six corporals, six bombardiers, six gunners and 28 matrosses – enough personnel to provide six crews (with attached infantry to move the guns) and an ammunition section. The Maryland companies had four officers and 102 enlisted men. Where possible, companies were armed with French-made brass 6-pdrs.

The artillery reflected Washington's demand that it be an integral part of the army, and not a separate body as in British service (although companies did follow British practice in serving a range of ordnance, according to need). Since the Trenton campaign, Knox had allocated one company – usually from the same state – to each infantry brigade for close support. He emphasized concentrated fire against enemy infantry (especially breaking up bayonet charges), rather than counter-battery duels. This meant that rate of fire and maneuverability in action were more important than range and so the 6-pdr became the preferred weapon, despite needing a 15-man crew. The brass guns used in the Monmouth campaign were much lighter than the homemade iron pieces or captured British guns of French and Indian War vintage used hitherto.

Militia

Almost all the militia units in the Monmouth campaign were from New Jersey, organized in county regiments, with individual companies drawn from neighboring towns and villages. The state's "minutemen" had been disbanded in 1776, but the militia still contained many French and Indian War veterans. Governor Livingston called out over 1,000 militia for 30 days' service from 1 May. By early June they had been replaced by a similar-sized contingent and these were the men who fought at Monmouth.

In addition, New Jersey had recruited numbers of militiamen to serve for nine months as State Troops (temporary, full-time units for local defense only, paid for by the state rather than Congress). In May 1778, these men were ordered to join the four Continental regiments, and by June they made up about 40 percent of the New Jersey line. New York and Maryland also used this method of bulking out their Continental regiments, and by June only the Massachusetts and North Carolina contingents did not include at least a few militia levies.

Finally, there is evidence that a few Pennsylvania militia joined Washington after the British evacuated Philadelphia, but their role (if any) on 28 June is unclear.

THE MONMOUTH COURTHOUSE CAMPAIGN

ENTER THE FRENCH

As the traditional enemy of Great Britain, France was the obvious choice as America's first ally. In November 1774, American agents had asked French diplomats in London for help and France had sent agents to England and America to gather intelligence. Covert aid (especially gunpowder) began arriving in 1776, via the French writer Beaumarchais and his ostensibly legitimate business, *Hortalez & Cie.* By September 1777, war matériel worth five million *livres* had reached America, along with several European officers (most of them French) seeking adventure and glory.

At Versailles, however, support for official involvement was far from unanimous. France faced an annual budget deficit of 20 million *livres* and much-needed reforms of the army and navy were far from finished. Spain, whose navy was essential to any maritime challenge to Great Britain, refused to join any alliance; the king, Carlos III, was not disposed to encourage colonial rebellion, whilst his ministers were nervous of American expansion in Louisiana. Tension between Austria-Hungary and Prussia over the Bavarian succession also threatened to make heavy demands on limited French military resources.

However, arguments for intervention were also persuasive – revenge, colonial expansion, and fears that if the rebellion ended soon (politically or militarily), British troops in America could attack the West Indies. The minor successes at Trenton and Princeton had impressed the French, but it was the victory at Saratoga that provided the catalyst for the alliance. Although it took the rest of Europe by surprise, France's Foreign Minister, the Comte de Vergennes, seized the opportunity to persuade Louis XVI to sign a formal treaty with the "United States of North America" on 6 February 1778. This implicit recognition of American independence led to an immediate breach of diplomatic relations and a declaration of war between Great Britain and France.

French involvement in the war had been expected in Great Britain, especially by the Royal Navy, which had kept its best ships and commanders in Europe. But while the war became more popular in Great Britain, the extra strain on limited resources led to a shift in strategy to total reliance on controlling each colony from a single military base on the coast, and on the emergence of those elusive Loyalist masses that ministers were convinced only needed a call to arms. On 8 March, Germain sent secret orders to reinforce the Caribbean and the Floridas, and to switch offensive operations from the interior, to the ports and harbors between New York City and Halifax. If necessary, Philadelphia should be evacuated to free up troops and another base established on the Delaware.

Louis XVI (1754-93) by Joseph Duplessis. Still only in the first year of his reign when war broke out, he was uncomfortable with encouraging colonial rebellion and undermining a fellow monarch – even that of France's great rival. Nonetheless, he was persuaded to sign the treaty of alliance by the pro-intervention lobby. (Chateau de Versailles)

Charles Gravier, Comte de Vergennes (1717–87) by Antoine Callet. Vergennes, together with the Minister of War, St Germain, and the Minister of Marine, Sartines, led the pro-war lobby within the French cabinet. (Chateau de Versailles)

Seeing the dangers of a war without allies and on several fronts, the Prime Minister, Lord North, sought a political end to the rebellion, leaving Great Britain free to fight France. On 17 February, he laid two Bills before Parliament: one removed all taxes and pledged to impose no more without the colonists' consent; the other established a Peace Commission, with powers to grant anything short of independence, to go to America and negotiate with Congress. Both Bills were passed and, on 22 April, three of the five commissioners – George Johnstone, Sir William Eden, and the leader, the Earl of Carlisle – boarded the *Trident* to sail to Philadelphia and join the other two (the Howe brothers).

The effect in America

Congress realized that it would be a while before France could send enough men and ships to North America to influence the course of the war. In the meantime, it was vital to maintain a level of military activity sufficient to reassure the French that the Americans did not now expect them to do all the fighting. Unfortunately, Congress and the Continental Army were facing problems that might reduce, or even end, their capacity to achieve this.

In 1777, Congress had recognized the inadequacies of its Board of War and replaced the civilian members with military officers – the Quartermaster General, Major General Thomas Mifflin; the Adjutant General, Colonel Timothy Pickering; and Washington's military secretary, Lieutenant Colonel Robert Harrison. Mifflin, a political opponent of Washington, recommended two more appointees – Major General Horatio Gates, the "victor" of Saratoga, as president, and Commissary General Joseph Trumbull. Mifflin and some like-minded members of Congress steered the vain but naive Gates into expanding the Board's role to include control of all military operations. Thomas Conway, an Irish officer in the French army and another critic of Washington, was promoted major general over the heads of several Americans, and then made Inspector General (in effect, a field agent for the Board). At the same time, an invasion of Canada – ostensibly led by Washington's favorite, the Marquis de La Fayette, but actually controlled by several of his opponents, including Conway – was planned without reference to the commander in chief.

Fortunately for Washington, the so-called Conway Cabal imploded on its own. Conway resigned and returned to France after being wounded in a duel. Gates resigned as president of the Board and returned to the Northern Department, La Fayette refused to lead the Canadian

View of log huts at Valley Forge. Over 1,000 huts were built, each measuring 16ft x 14ft (4.9m x 4.2m) and housing one squad. Modern research suggests that nobody froze or starved to death, that morale was high (as it would had to have been for such a feat of construction in the depths of winter), and that between December 1777 and February 1778, enough flour, meat, and fish was delivered to give each man 6lbs of food per day. (Author's photograph)

expedition, forcing its abandonment, and Mifflin was investigated over financial irregularities. By May 1778, the Board was reduced to a purely administrative body, and Washington was once more unchallenged in relation to military policy.

As if all this was not enough, the Continental Army was in a poor state. In December 1777, Washington had moved the Main Army to Valley Forge, 22 miles (35km) from Philadelphia by wagon road; close enough to remain a threat, but safe from British raids. By January 1778, the severe weather had highlighted the shortage of food and clothing and Washington was forced to requisition grain from local farmers. On paper, he should have had 60,000 troops; in reality there were barely 20,000, of whom 5,000 were sick, 11,000 were on furlough, and 3,000 more were unfit for duty through lack of shoes or clothes. Junior officers were resigning for economic reasons, as the Continental Army had no equivalent to the British purchase and half-pay systems. Another problem lay in ensuring that every officer and enlisted man was familiar with whatever standard drill the new Board of War decided to adopt. Unfortunately, there was no standard drill and Congress had no obvious candidate to produce one and oversee its introduction.

In February 1778, matters took a turn for the better with the arrival at Valley Forge of a former Prussian officer, "Baron" Friedrich von Steuben. Steuben took the unofficial British regulations of 1764, already known to many units, and adapted them by introducing elements of French or Prussian drill that accommodated the qualities and short-comings of the American soldier, such as faster movement (75 paces per minute instead of 60). He taught the use of the bayonet, replaced single file with close columns, and introduced skirmish screens to protect the line of march. He also divided large regiments or consolidated smaller ones in order to establish a standard-size battalion. The changes were introduced via a "model" company of 100 men drawn from every brigade in the Main Army who, along with a select group of officers, were sent back to their units to pass on these new skills.

As his army became more professional, Washington considered how best to use it. On 20 April, he asked his generals to consider three

Washington's headquarters (Isaac Potts' house) at Valley Forge. This building was home and office to Washington and over 20 staff officers for six months. The area around the house had been the center of a thriving iron industry (giving the valley its name) until a British raid in September 1777. (Author's photograph)

Major General Baron Friedrich Wilhelm Augustus von Steuben (1730–94) by C.W. Peale. Steuben was born into a military family and joined the Prussian Army at 17. He had ten years' experience drilling infantry before becoming a regimental staff officer in a *Frei Korps*. In 1762, he became an aide to Frederick the Great and, like Charles Lee, spent some time in Russia before army politics forced his retirement. He spent a decade as chamberlain to a minor, bankrupt, German prince, and was unemployed when recommended to Franklin by the French Minister of War, St Germain. (Independence National Historical Park)

options for future action: attacking Philadelphia; attacking New York City; or remaining at Valley Forge to continue training and recruiting. His brigadier generals (all Americans) favored either the first or second option. One of his American major generals, William Alexander (also known as Lord Stirling), suggested doing both; the other – Nathanael Greene – proposed leaving most of the troops at Valley Forge and attacking New York City with 4,000 picked men and the New England militia. Only the foreign officers – La Fayette, Steuben and Du Portail – recommended the third option; interestingly, this was the one Washington eventually chose.

Three days later, Lee arrived at Valley Forge, but left immediately to lobby Congress (now sitting at York, Pennsylvania) and did not return until 20 May. On 6 May, news of the alliance with France was greeted with a *feu de joie* and two days later, another council of war confirmed the decision to await events; on 11 May, all the officers of the Continental Army swore a new oath of allegiance. It was now an open secret that the British were preparing to leave Philadelphia and Washington sent a brigade of Continentals into New Jersey to harass them if they went by land – increasingly seen as the most likely option. On 2 June, he warned the commander of the New Jersey militia, Brigadier General Philamon Dickinson, to stay alert to British movements and help Greene – the new Quartermaster General – to collect and store the supplies the Main Army might need on a march through New Jersey.

In Philadelphia, the King's forces had their own problems. The popular view of the British living in luxury, gambling, drinking, and attending the theatre whilst the Continentals froze and starved just 20 miles away, might have been true for a handful of officers. For the rest, however, and still more so for the rank-and-file, the winter of 1777 saw similar shortages to those at Valley Forge, and morale and discipline suffered accordingly. Yet despite these difficulties, Sir William Howe was widely – and probably unfairly – criticized for not attacking Valley Forge. Aware that disease and desertion were rife in Washington's army, he may have believed that there was no point in losing men that he could not replace, when nature was doing his job for him. In any event, assembling a force large enough to guarantee success would have meant virtually abandoning the city, and would also have been impossible to keep secret. Valley Forge was a day's march in good weather; in winter, it would have taken several days and the local roads could not have coped with so many men, horses, and vehicles. By the time the roads were passable again, Washington had strengthened his defenses.

France's entry into the war almost reversed Howe's and Washington's positions. Philadelphia was vulnerable to blockade since all supplies and reinforcements had to come by water. A journey from New York City – just 100 miles away – required a 200-mile voyage, one half of it along a stretch of coast renowned for its storms, the other up a river with many natural obstacles and which (in theory if not in practice) could be controlled by enemy shore batteries. Quite apart from any forces sent from Europe, France had a large Caribbean fleet that could descend on the east coast of America with little or no warning, making Philadelphia a trap for both naval and land forces.

As the spring thaw came, the *petite guerre* (the war of outposts, foraging, raids, and ambushes) resumed. Between 18 and 21 March, a force led by

Colonel Charles Mawhood (17th, 27th and 46th Foot, the Queen's Rangers and the New Jersey Volunteers) crossed the Delaware and attacked New Jersey militia units at Quintan's Bridge and Hancock's Bridge, near Salem. On 1 May, another raiding party (the 1st Light Infantry, some light dragoons, and the Queen's Rangers) almost captured Brigadier General John Lacey of the Pennsylvania militia at Crooked Billet. Six days later, the 2nd Light Infantry, in two row galleys and some flatboats, attacked American shipping near Bordentown, destroying two frigates of 32 and 28 guns, three 16-gun privateers, 23 brigs, and several sloops, as well as the homes of prominent militia officers.

By now, Sir William Howe had learned that he had been recalled to England and Sir Henry Clinton would succeed him as commander in chief in North America. Clinton arrived in Philadelphia from New York City on 8 May, and three days later Howe informed the army of the change in command (Lord Howe decided to await his successor and, fortunately for British arms, remained in America until September). Sir William Howe's popularity – in America, at least – was demonstrated on 18 May by the flamboyant *Meschianza* organized by a group of his officers and attended by the cream of military and civilian society. During the event, word reached Philadelphia that Washington had sent La Fayette across the Schuykill River with 2,200 men and five guns, to gather information on British plans for evacuation and to disrupt their foraging parties.

Aware of La Fayette's inexperience and his desperate desire to lead troops into battle, Washington provided detailed orders and assigned him Brigadier General Enoch Poor's Brigade, veterans of Saratoga. La Fayette crossed Swede's Ford on 18 May and camped at Barren Hill, halfway between the opposing armies. Poor's infantry and the five guns were on top of the hill, their right protected by steep cliffs and their left by three stone houses, a church and a cemetery. On the forward slope were 150 rangers and 50 Oneida warriors, under Major Allen McLane, while 600 Pennsylvania militia under Brigadier General James Potter covered the road from Whitemarsh.

Lieutenant-General Sir William Howe. By 1778, Howe was clearly weary of a war that he had been unable to end, either as a general or as a peace negotiator. He returned to England to find himself blamed for Burgoyne's defeat and accused of prolonging the war for his own financial ends. (National Army Museum)

Brigadier-General the Honourable Alexander Leslie (1740–94) by Thomas Gainsborough. Leslie joined the 3rd Foot Guards in 1753 and was lieutenant-colonel of the 64th Foot in Boston in 1775. From 1776, he commanded a brigade and served competently, if unspectacularly, in the New York and Philadelphia campaigns. (Private collection)

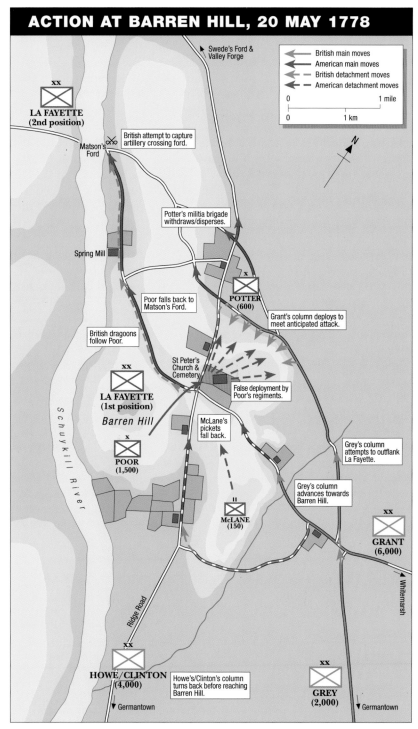

ACTION AT BARREN HILL, 20 MAY 1778

	British main moves
	American main moves
	British detachment moves
	American detachment moves

0   1 mile
0   1 km

Swede's Ford & Valley Forge

LA FAYETTE (2nd position)

Matson's Ford

British attempt to capture artillery crossing ford.

Potter's militia brigade withdraws/disperses.

Spring Mill

POTTER (600)

Poor falls back to Matson's Ford.

Grant's column deploys to meet anticipated attack.

British dragoons follow Poor.

LA FAYETTE (1st position)

Barren Hill

St Peter's Church & Cemetery

False deployment by Poor's regiments.

POOR (1,500)

McLane's pickets fall back.

Grey's column attempts to outflank La Fayette.

Grey's column advances towards Barren Hill.

McLANE (150)

GRANT (6,000)

Schuylkill River

Ridge Road

Whitemarsh

HOWE/CLINTON (4,000)

Howe's/Clinton's column turns back before reaching Barren Hill.

GREY (2,000)

Germantown

Germantown

Perhaps seeing one last chance for glory before going home, Howe mobilized virtually his entire army. Major-General James Grant left the city after dark on 19 May, with 6,000 men and 15 guns, with orders to circle behind La Fayette and block his retreat. Howe and Clinton led 4,000 men north from Germantown, to pin La Fayette in front, whilst Major-General Charles Grey took 2,000 British and Hessian grenadiers to hit the Frenchman's left. All three columns were to attack early on the morning of 20 May.

Unfortunately, the capture of two of Grey's grenadiers alerted La Fayette, whilst Grant's decision to halt and await Grey's arrival gave the Frenchman time to fall back to Matson's Ford at the foot of Barren Hill, via a narrow track not known to the British. La Fayette ordered the heads of Poor's regiments to make a feint toward the church, causing Grant's column to halt a second time, whilst the main bodies and the artillery moved down to the ford. Grant eventually became aware of the ruse and sent some cavalry after the Americans, but not knowing the area, they took a long route and only arrived in time to skirmish ineffectually with La Fayette's rearguard as it crossed the Schuykill. Thwarted, Howe turned his columns around and they straggled back into Philadelphia throughout the remainder of a hot day, Grant's men having marched over 30 miles. (The story that Howe planned a dinner to display a captive La Fayette is apocryphal, and probably arose from confusion over invitations to the *Meschianza*.)

Three days after the Barren Hill debacle, and two days before Sir William Howe left for England in the frigate *Andromeda*, Clinton received the orders sent by Lord Germain in March. He decided almost immediately to ignore the instruction to evacuate by sea and instead planned to march across New Jersey – either directly to New York City via New Brunswick, or overland to Sandy Hook, completing the journey by sea. Apart from the threat of being trapped in the Delaware, or caught in the open sea, by a French fleet, he simply did not have enough transports to carry almost 20,000 troops, their artillery, baggage, and wives and children, and those Loyalist civilians desperate to escape the wrath of their fellow colonists. This plan required an enormous wagon train, capable of carrying everything that could not go by sea, and enough provisions and military supplies for the march (estimated at two weeks). Such a train would be slow and difficult to defend, especially against troops who knew the country; but if he could obtain enough of a head start, Clinton believed it could be done.

Major-General James Grant (1720-1806) by John Kay. Grant was famed for his vehement anti-American views and consistently poor performance on the battlefield. His refusal to obey an order from Clinton on 28 June may account for his being sent to the West Indies later that year. (National Portrait Gallery)

The "Indian King" tavern in Haddonfield. The tavern in King Street was Clinton's headquarters on the night of 18/19 June. (Author's photograph)

However, his plans were brought to an abrupt halt on 6 June, when the Peace Commissioners arrived in Philadelphia. On 13 June, they contacted Congress explaining their mission and offering several concessions, including freedom from external legislation and recognition of local assemblies. These might have been acceptable in 1776, but now they were seen for what they were, an act of desperation. Congress demanded either full independence, or the removal of all Royal forces from North America, as a pre-condition of negotiation.

The Commissioners received an equally frosty response from Clinton's army and the Loyalists – both equally outraged at the concessions offered (not to mention having expected 20,000 more troops rather than three civilians). Clinton was also upset at having to postpone the evacuation, which the Commissioners saw as weakening their negotiating position; in contrast, military leaders on both sides believed that the delay made it harder for Clinton when he did leave. Both sides continued to correspond until August, when Congress resolved never to negotiate, and in November the three Commissioners returned to London, having met no one and achieved nothing.

TWO ROADS TO MONMOUTH

During May, the chief British engineer, Captain John Montresor, had built defensive works at Cooper's Ferry on the New Jersey side of the Delaware. Ostensibly, the post was there to cover woodcutting parties, but on 28 May, all pretence ceased when it was heavily reinforced; the next day, the post's commander, Brigadier-General Alexander Leslie, reported enemy militia gathering around him. By 10 June, some 1,500 baggage wagons had been sent across along with further reinforcements.

Meanwhile, the men too sick to march had been embarked on transports, along with the women and children (only two women per company could march with the army), 3,000 Loyalist refugees, and the suspect Anspach-Bayreuth troops. Over the next five days, Leslie received all the field artillery and officers' horses, and Loos' Hessian Brigade. On 16 June, the cavalry crossed over with Lieutenant-General Wilhelm von Knyphausen and Major-General James Grant, the Hessian Grenadiers, the Jägers, and the remaining Loyalist corps. The stage was now set for the evacuation.

Clinton's march
On 17 June, the troops in Philadelphia paraded at 6.00pm, before proceeding to the outer defenses, where they slept on their arms. At 3.00am the next day the transports left, followed eight hours later by Howe's fleet, which had protected the troops as they crossed from Gloucester into New Jersey. Other than a few enemy horsemen who entered the city as the troops left, no enemy forces were seen. At 11.00am, Clinton's main body marched to Haddonfield, where it joined Knyphausen's contingent from Cooper's Ferry, and the entire force camped for the night, apart from some light troops who pushed on to Foster's Town.

On 19 June, Clinton left Haddonfield at dawn, but only covered six miles before heavy rain forced him to halt at Evesham for the rest of the

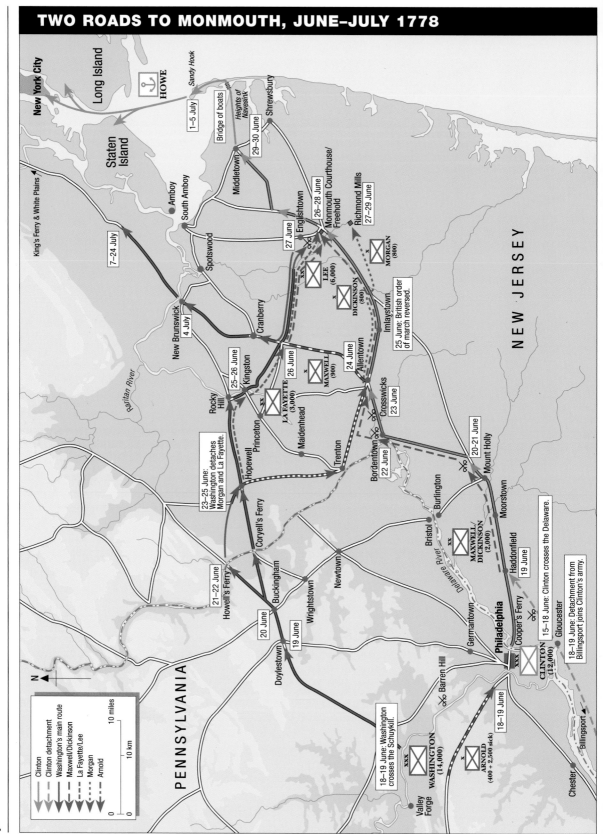

day. The 28th and 55th Foot were sent to retrieve the Billingsport garrison and, whilst awaiting their return, Knyphausen used the time to move the baggage train and artillery park over a deep ravine that crossed the road a mile and a half beyond Haddonfield. The next day, Clinton left Evesham about 5.00am, but heavy rain turned the sandy roads to clay and limited progress to just seven miles. He halted at Mount Holly (a good defensive position abandoned by Maxwell the previous morning) and some jägers in Leslie's advance guard skirmished with the militia. At the same time Knyphausen advanced through open country to Moorestown, arriving around 9.00am[1].

Clinton spent 21 June at Mount Holly, whilst Knyphausen brought up the baggage via Chester and encamped in the rear of Cornwallis's division. The army rested for the remainder of the day, and Cornwallis amended his order of march. He brought his light troops and pioneers to the front of the column, to counter militia efforts to impede the retreat by dismantling bridges and felling trees across roads[2]. Clinton and Cornwallis left Mount Holly at 3.00am on 22 June, followed by the baggage and artillery, and finally Knyphausen's division, which departed at 6.00am. The countryside became more open, but both divisions had to use the same road, with Leslie's Brigade protecting their left. That afternoon, the entire force camped near Black Horse tavern, which Clinton made his headquarters. There he learned that Maxwell's Brigade had only left at 2.00am and leaflets were found warning him against "being Burgoyned".

Hanging a deserter. On 20 June, several militia were captured, including a former drummer of the 28th Foot who had deserted. He was executed on 23 June and left hanging at the roadside as a warning. (Private collection)

---

1 Order of march for Knyphausen's division from 20 June: (1) 200 British light infantry and a detachment of the 17th Light Dragoons; (2) 1st and 2nd Brigades; (3) Stirn's and Loos' brigades, and the Hessian Grenadiers; (4) the park of artillery, provision train, and baggage; (5) a rearguard of one British and one Hessian regiment and the 16th Light Dragoons. Flank guards were provided by the 10th Foot, and the Maryland Loyalists and Roman Catholic Volunteers.

2 Order of march for Cornwallis's division from 22 June: (1) 90 mounted and all the dismounted jagers; (2) the Queen's Rangers; (3) one officer and 20 pioneers; (4) 1st Light Infantry; (5) 60 pioneers and two wagons with their tools; (6) 16th Light Dragoons; (7) British and Hessian Grenadiers; (8) two 12-pdrs and a 5½-in. howitzer; (9) Foot Guards; (10) 3rd Brigade; (11) 4th Brigade, less one battalion as left flank guard; (12) six pontoons and the rest of the engineer's tools; (13) all the bat horses and baggage; (14) cattle; (15) 5th Brigade and Hovenden's cavalry.

Harassing Clinton's column. Amongst Dickinson's militia were 25 men who were employed solely in felling trees across the roads. Other groups removed the planking from bridges and filled up wells. (Private collection)

On 23 June, Clinton once again split his army into two columns; Knyphausen on the right with the baggage, Cornwallis on the left led by Leslie's Brigade. Cornwallis left at 4.00am, marching four miles to the Rising Sun tavern and then three miles to Crosswicks. At Recklesstown Creek, 50 militia occupying a mill fled as Leslie's advance guard appeared, but later exchanged shots with the main body as it approached Crosswicks Creek. They then withdrew across the creek, destroying the bridge, and joined more militia on the far bank. The Queen's Rangers charged across and dispersed them, losing an officer and five men wounded. Some of the militia barricaded themselves in the local meetinghouse, but withdrew when the 1st Light Infantry brought up a 3-pdr. Once the bridge was repaired, some light dragoons and light infantry pursued the militia for two miles toward Allentown until halted by another damaged bridge. Cornwallis continued his march to Crosswicks, whilst

The Friends' Meetinghouse in Crosswicks. The building is virtually unchanged; the interior woodwork still bears the marks of Hessian bayonets, and a 3-pdr ball remains embedded in the upper wall. (Author's photograph)

A close-up of the Friends' Meetinghouse in Crosswicks. The 3-pdr ball can still be seen embedded in the wall between the two upper floor windows (the light colored "dot" just below the right hand shutter of the left-hand window. (Author's photograph)

Leslie pushed on to Bordentown, where artillery in an earthwork by Bordentown Creek fired on him.

The next day, Leslie crossed the creek and marched through Bordentown, exchanging shots with militia attempting to destroy a drawbridge. He rejoined Cornwallis around 6.00am and the entire division marched four miles to Allentown. Meanwhile, Knyphausen had left Recklesstown at 4.00am, halting to repair the bridge over Crosswicks Creek. By noon, his division was across and heading for Imlaystown, where they spent the night. Once Clinton knew Knyphausen was safe, he left Crosswicks for Allentown.

Clinton had two possible routes to New York City – via Sandy Hook, completing his journey by sea, or overland across the Raritan River and into the city via Staten Island or the Hudson River ferries. Now he had to choose and he selected Sandy Hook, because his army was running short of provisions and that route was shorter and passed through defensible country. The alternative route led through areas where it would be difficult to forage, and where he could be trapped between Washington and Gates. Accordingly, Knyphausen's division left Imlaystown at 4.00am on 25 June, heading northeast rather than northwest. Two hours later, Clinton left Allentown whilst Leslie headed south to join the rear of Knyphausen's column. Anticipating that any attacks would now focus on the rear of his column, rather than the front, Cornwallis reversed his order of march. The army halted for three hours just after noon, before Knyphausen's division continued to Thompson's Meetinghouse and Cornwallis's division to the Rising Sun tavern.

On 26 June, Knyphausen's division marched four miles to Monmouth Courthouse, arriving just after 9.00am, and camped about a mile farther on. Around 10.00am, Cornwallis's division arrived and occupied high ground to the west of the courthouse on the Allentown road, with small contingents covering the Englishtown and Amboy roads. Skirmishing continued throughout the day, but nightfall brought heavy thunder and rain that lasted until the next morning. The rain and subsequent heat kept Clinton's army inactive after midday on 26 June and throughout the following day, despite the reported proximity of several enemy formations. Militia parties were observed hovering around the outer pickets and some British and Hessian foragers were captured after straying too far beyond the lines. That afternoon, Clinton planned the next stage of his march. After learning from his Quartermaster General, Sir William Erskine, that enemy forces were operating around his preferred route, he decided to send both divisions along a more northerly road, toward Middletown, with Knyphausen leaving at 3.00am and Cornwallis at 5.00am. The night of 27 June was even hotter and more thundery and both divisions lay on their arms.

Washington's response

On 17 June, as Clinton prepared to leave Philadelphia, Washington held another council of war at Valley Forge, asking his generals what they should do when the British left. The replies showed that they were still divided, with the "foreign" officers (Lee, Steuben, and Du Portail) still opposed to a general engagement, and the Americans (and La Fayette) in favor of offensive action – the degree of aggression advised reflecting each officer's own character. The following morning, scouting parties

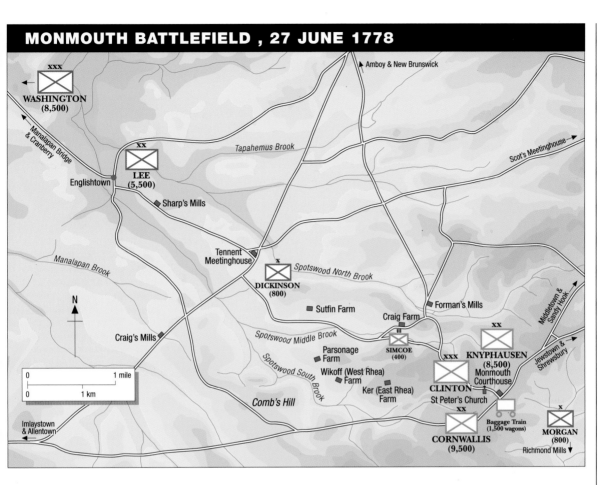

MONMOUTH BATTLEFIELD , 27 JUNE 1778

WASHINGTON (8,500)

Manalapan Bridge & Cranberry

Amboy & New Brunswick

Tapahemus Brook

Scot's Meetinghouse

LEE (5,500)

Englishtown

Sharp's Mills

Manalapan Brook

Tennent Meetinghouse

Spotswood North Brook

DICKINSON (800)

Sutfin Farm

Forman's Mills

Craig Farm

N

Craig's Mills

Spotswood Middle Brook

Parsonage Farm

SIMCOE (400)

KNYPHAUSEN (8,500) Monmouth Courthouse

Middletown & Sandy Hook

Spotswood South Brook

Wikoff (West Rhea) Farm

Ker (East Rhea) Farm

CLINTON St Peter's Church

Jewstown & Shrewsbury

Comb's Hill

Imlaystown & Allentown

CORNWALLIS (9,500)

Baggage Train (1,500 wagons)

MORGAN (800)

Richmond Mills

0 — 1 mile
0 — 1 km

entered Philadelphia to find the British gone (or at least most of them – McLane captured two groups of stragglers). As the information filtered back to his headquarters, Washington began amending the general movement orders that he had prepared in May. Two divisions would march on the first day, two more the next, and the last – with the baggage and artillery – on the third day[3]. These intervals would be kept to avoid crowding on the roads and troops would move out by 4.00am to complete a full march before the hottest part of the day. Afternoons would be spent cooking meals and preparing for the next day's march. The front and right flank of the army would be covered by mounted troops, and each regiment would provide flank guards (a sergeant and 12 privates for every 200 enlisted men).

At 3.00pm, Lee's division left Valley Forge and Wayne's division followed at 5.00pm, being joined en route by a corps under Colonel Daniel

[3] The order of march of the Continental Army from Valley Forge:
1st Division (Major General Charles Lee)
Poor's, Varnum's and Huntington's brigades
2nd Division (Brigadier General Anthony Wayne vice Major General Thomas Mifflin absent)
1st Pennsylvania, 2nd Pennsylvania, and late Conway's brigades
3rd Division (Major General the Marquis de La Fayette)
Woodford's, Scott's and North Carolina brigades
4th Division (Major General Baron Johann de Kalb absent sick)
Glover's, Patterson's and Learned's brigades
The artillery park and spare ammunition
5th Division (Major General William Alexander, Lord Stirling)
Muhlenberg's, late Weedon's, 1st Maryland and 2nd Maryland brigades
The baggage of the army

Morgan. Both Lee (in overall command) and Wayne were to proceed to Coryell's Ferry, cross and then halt on the first defensible ground to await the main body. However, the late start meant that neither division covered more than three miles; both crossed the Schuykill then halted for the night, before reaching the Delaware late the next day.

On 19 June, Washington led his main body out of Valley Forge, through heavy rain along the York road to Doylestown, where he spent the night. The same day, he appointed Benedict Arnold governor of Philadelphia, with instructions to re-establish control and to prepare inventories of all useful goods and supplies, and particularly the property of any Loyalists. Colonel Philip Van Cortlandt was left at Valley Forge, with the 3,000 men considered too sick to march (2,500 of whom followed Arnold to Philadelphia, leaving the 500 worst cases in camp).

On 20 June, Lee and Wayne crossed the Delaware at Coryell's Ferry and marched three miles, while Washington moved his headquarters to Buckingham, from where he wrote to Gates informing him of events. Late the next day, Washington crossed the Delaware at Coryell's Ferry and Howell's Ferry (three miles upriver). Having covered 40 miles (64km) in three days, he allowed the army to rest on 22 June and spent the day writing reports to Congress. He also ordered his troops to leave behind their tents and heavy baggage, guarded by those no longer fit to march, and instructed each brigade to send an officer and 25 marksmen to join Morgan. He also reorganized the army into two wings and a reserve to simplify the order of march [4]. By 23 June, his entire force was camped at Hopewell, 14 miles north of Trenton. That same morning, Brigadier General John Cadwalader of the Pennsylvania militia, left Philadelphia with 400 Continentals, 100 militia volunteers and several wagon loads of much-needed cartridges.

At 9.00am on 24 June, during a solar eclipse, Washington called a council of war. He informed the meeting of the movements, location and strength of the enemy, and of his own forces (which were approximately equal), and asked their views on precipitating a general engagement. Lee argued that it was better to allow Clinton to leave New Jersey, since the alliance with France would do more to hasten independence than anything they could achieve in a single battle. Only a minor reinforcement, if that, should be sent to Maxwell and Dickinson. Several generals agreed with Lee, but Greene, Wayne, and La Fayette wanted a large detachment sent out immediately, with the main body kept within striking distance. Eventually, the council (including a reluctant Lee) agreed. After some thought, Washington sent Morgan and 600 men to help Maxwell harass the British right flank and rear, and 1,500 picked men under Brigadier General Charles Scott to do the same to their left. He then instructed Steuben to reconnoiter the area and gather intelligence to divine which route Clinton would take.

The next day, Washington moved his entire force to Rocky Hill and Kingston from where he sent a third force (another 1,000 picked men led by Wayne) to annoy the enemy. Alongside Wayne went La Fayette, who

Aaron Burr (1756–1836) by John Vanderlyn. Burr commanded a detachment of Malcolm's Additional Regiment, in the brigade formerly led by Conway. During Wayne's attack at the end of the day, Burr's horse was killed under him – a fate he shared that day with Alexander Hamilton, the man he would later kill in a duel. (New York Historical Society)

Colonel Daniel Morgan (1736–1802) by C.W. Peale. Morgan's first completely independent command was not a success, perhaps due in part to his inexperience, but probably more to a lack of communication from his superiors. (Independence National Historical Park)

---

4 The order of march of the Continental Army from Coryell's Ferry:
Right wing (Major General Charles Lee) –
Woodford's, Scott's North Carolina, Poor's, Varnum's, and Huntington's brigades
Left wing (Major General Lord Stirling) –
1st Pennsylvania, 2nd Pennsylvania, late Conway's, Glover's, Patterson's, and Learned's brigades
Reserve (Major General the Marquis de La Fayette) –
1st Maryland, 2nd Maryland, Muhlenberg's, late Weedon's, and (on joining) Maxwell's brigades

would take overall charge of the independent commands now harassing the enemy, totaling almost 5,000 men. As second-in-command the post should have been offered to Lee, but his negative views (expressed after, as well as during, the council of war) forced Washington to overlook him. For his part, Lee remarked that he was happy to be free of responsibility for a plan he was sure would fail. However, during the night of 24 June, Lee reconsidered his position, and the following evening asked Washington for command of all the detached corps, arguing that a refusal would inevitably result in disgrace. Washington considered the request whilst the army marched from Rocky Hill to Cranberry on the evening of 25 June. Bad weather kept the army there all the next day, but allowed Washington to find a solution. By adding more troops to La Fayette's division, Washington made it large enough to require a more senior officer in charge. This answer saved La Fayette's face and placated Lee.

The additional force comprised the remainder of Scott's and Varnum's brigades, united under Colonel William Grayson. At the same time Washington sent orders to all advanced detachments to rendezvous with Lee at Englishtown. By now Lee had over 5,500 men, including another 200 Continentals just arrived from Philadelphia under Colonel Henry Jackson. As Lee reviewed the troops on the high ground a mile west of Englishtown Creek, he told an aide that he hardly knew any of the officers under him.

On 27 June, Washington marched from Cranberry to Manalapan Bridge, and that afternoon he rode to Englishtown for a council of war at which he expressed his desire that the army should attack Clinton the following morning. He then returned to Manalapan, leaving Lee to assemble his own subordinates for what turned out to be a very brief meeting (Scott, arriving 30 minutes late, had found everyone gone). Lee told them he had no reliable intelligence on the exact location and strength of the enemy, or the ground they might fight over. With so many unknowns it was difficult to formulate a plan there and then, and he asked that they all serve as required and not dispute rank, or posts of honor. He then wrote to Dickinson that he would attack once the British were on the move, but that Dickinson must tell him when this occurred.

On his way back to Mananlapan Bridge, Washington had noted how vulnerable Lee's troops might be to a sudden attack and sent an aide, Lieutenant Colonel John Fitzgerald, to inform Lee of this, and ask him to

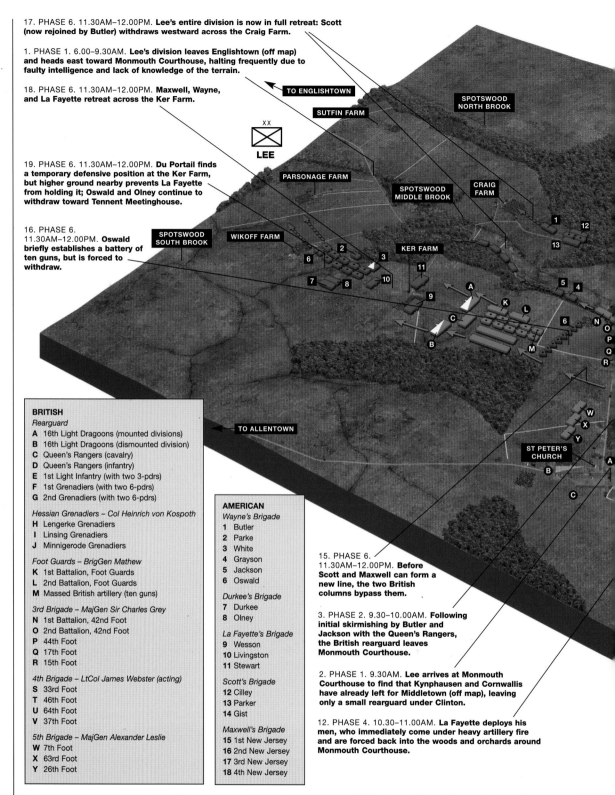

17. PHASE 6. 11.30AM–12.00PM. **Lee's entire division is now in full retreat:** Scott (now rejoined by Butler) withdraws westward across the Craig Farm.

1. PHASE 1. 6.00–9.30AM. **Lee's division leaves Englishtown (off map)** and heads east toward Monmouth Courthouse, halting frequently due to faulty intelligence and lack of knowledge of the terrain.

18. PHASE 6. 11.30AM–12.00PM. **Maxwell, Wayne, and La Fayette** retreat across the Ker Farm.

19. PHASE 6. 11.30AM–12.00PM. **Du Portail finds** a temporary defensive position at the Ker Farm, but higher ground nearby prevents La Fayette from holding it; Oswald and Olney continue to withdraw toward Tennent Meetinghouse.

16. PHASE 6. 11.30AM–12.00PM. **Oswald** briefly establishes a battery of ten guns, but is forced to withdraw.

TO ENGLISHTOWN

SPOTSWOOD NORTH BROOK

SUTFIN FARM

XX
LEE

PARSONAGE FARM

SPOTSWOOD MIDDLE BROOK

CRAIG FARM

SPOTSWOOD SOUTH BROOK

WIKOFF FARM

KER FARM

TO ALLENTOWN

ST PETER'S CHURCH

BRITISH
Rearguard
A   16th Light Dragoons (mounted divisions)
B   16th Light Dragoons (dismounted division)
C   Queen's Rangers (cavalry)
D   Queen's Rangers (infantry)
E   1st Light Infantry (with two 3-pdrs)
F   1st Grenadiers (with two 6-pdrs)
G   2nd Grenadiers (with two 6-pdrs)

Hessian Grenadiers – Col Heinrich von Kospoth
H   Lengerke Grenadiers
I   Linsing Grenadiers
J   Minnigerode Grenadiers

Foot Guards – BrigGen Mathew
K   1st Battalion, Foot Guards
L   2nd Battalion, Foot Guards
M   Massed British artillery (ten guns)

3rd Brigade – MajGen Sir Charles Grey
N   1st Battalion, 42nd Foot
O   2nd Battalion, 42nd Foot
P   44th Foot
Q   17th Foot
R   15th Foot

4th Brigade – LtCol James Webster (acting)
S   33rd Foot
T   46th Foot
U   64th Foot
V   37th Foot

5th Brigade – MajGen Alexander Leslie
W   7th Foot
X   63rd Foot
Y   26th Foot

AMERICAN
Wayne's Brigade
1   Butler
2   Parke
3   White
4   Grayson
5   Jackson
6   Oswald

Durkee's Brigade
7   Durkee
8   Olney

La Fayette's Brigade
9   Wesson
10 Livingston
11 Stewart

Scott's Brigade
12 Cilley
13 Parker
14 Gist

Maxwell's Brigade
15 1st New Jersey
16 2nd New Jersey
17 3rd New Jersey
18 4th New Jersey

15. PHASE 6. 11.30AM–12.00PM. **Before Scott and Maxwell can form a new line, the two British columns bypass them.**

3. PHASE 2. 9.30–10.00AM. **Following initial skirmishing by Butler and Jackson with the Queen's Rangers, the British rearguard leaves Monmouth Courthouse.**

2. PHASE 1. 9.30AM. **Lee arrives at Monmouth Courthouse to find that Kynphausen and Cornwallis have already left for Middletown (off map), leaving only a small rearguard under Clinton.**

12. PHASE 4. 10.30–11.00AM. **La Fayette deploys his men, who immediately come under heavy artillery fire and are forced back into the woods and orchards around Monmouth Courthouse.**

MONMOUTH COURTHOUSE – LEE'S ADVANCE

Sunday, 28 June 1778, 6.00am–12.00pm, viewed from the southeast, showing the abortive attack by Lee's Division on the British rearguard, and Clinton's counterattack.

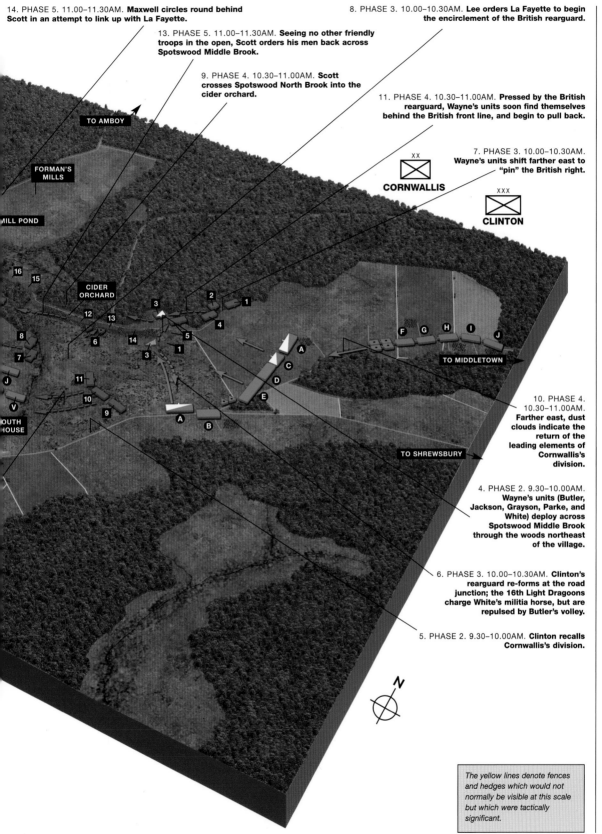

14. PHASE 5. 11.00–11.30AM. **Maxwell circles round behind Scott in an attempt to link up with La Fayette.**

13. PHASE 5. 11.00–11.30AM. **Seeing no other friendly troops in the open, Scott orders his men back across Spotswood Middle Brook.**

9. PHASE 4. 10.30–11.00AM. **Scott crosses Spotswood North Brook into the cider orchard.**

8. PHASE 3. 10.00–10.30AM. **Lee orders La Fayette to begin the encirclement of the British rearguard.**

11. PHASE 4. 10.30–11.00AM. **Pressed by the British rearguard, Wayne's units soon find themselves behind the British front line, and begin to pull back.**

7. PHASE 3. 10.00–10.30AM. **Wayne's units shift farther east to "pin" the British right.**

TO AMBOY

FORMAN'S MILLS

MILL POND

CORNWALLIS

CLINTON

CIDER ORCHARD

16

15

12   13

8

7

6

14

J

V

11

10

9

OUTH HOUSE

3

2   1

4

5

1

3

A

B

A

C

D

E

F G H I J

TO MIDDLETOWN

10. PHASE 4. 10.30–11.00AM. **Farther east, dust clouds indicate the return of the leading elements of Cornwallis's division.**

TO SHREWSBURY

4. PHASE 2. 9.30–10.00AM. **Wayne's units (Butler, Jackson, Grayson, Parke, and White) deploy across Spotswood Middle Brook through the woods northeast of the village.**

6. PHASE 3. 10.00–10.30AM. **Clinton's rearguard re-forms at the road junction; the 16th Light Dragoons charge White's militia horse, but are repulsed by Butler's volley.**

5. PHASE 2. 9.30–10.00AM. **Clinton recalls Cornwallis's division.**

N

The yellow lines denote fences and hedges which would not normally be visible at this scale but which were tactically significant.

keep Dickinson and Morgan informed of his plans. Lee told Fitzgerald that a message was on its way to Dickinson, but that he had no idea where Morgan was. Later that evening, Washington sent Lee another message warning that Clinton might move early in the morning, or even during the night, and that Lee should keep 600 to 800 men in close contact with the enemy to "pin" the enemy's rearguard until Lee could bring up the main part of his division. The letter added that Morgan was south of the current British line of march and should be brought into similar proximity to the enemy.

Lee received this message in the early hours of 28 June. He promptly ordered Dickinson to move nearer to the British outposts and observe their movements and informed Grayson that his detachment would lead the division the next morning. Finally, Lee sent Morgan a letter giving him discretion to attack the enemy as soon as they began to move. Unfortunately, the wording of the letter (written around midnight) may have led Morgan to believe that Lee would attack on the morning of 29 June, rather than 28 June, and he seems to have acted accordingly, leaving Lee's right flank unprotected throughout the coming day.

MONMOUTH COURTHOUSE – THE MORNING ACTION

At 3.00am, Lee ordered Grayson to lead his 600-man detachment through Englishtown toward Monmouth Courthouse. Grayson's men left their coats and packs in camp on the heights west of Englishtown and arrived at Lee's headquarters around 6:00am. Grayson had expected to be met by guides that Lee's aide, Captain Evan Edwards, had arranged to accompany him, but they did not appear. Eventually, General David Forman arrived at Lee's headquarters; Forman lived in the area and knew who could be trusted and he led Grayson out of Englishtown.

Some time around 5.00am, Lee had received a message from Dickinson, timed at 4.30am, that the British were moving out of Monmouth Courthouse toward Middletown. Lee promptly ordered the rest of his division to march, but it was 7.00am before the first units were

Brigadier General Anthony Wayne (1745–96) by J. Sharples. Despite his rank, Wayne's reputation was such that he was given command of Mifflin's division on the march from Valley Forge, and later one of the brigades of "picked men" assigned to Lee. Always ready for action, his disdain for those who were more cautious bordered on zealotry and he became Lee's main critic. (Independence National Historical Park)

The Covenhoven House outside Freehold. This house, owned by 74-year-old Elizabeth Covenhoven, was Clinton's headquarters from 26 to 28 June. The Allentown road was later "moved" and now passes to the west of the house, hence this face – the original front – is now at the rear. (Author's photograph)

OPPOSITE **The Tennent Meetinghouse today. The church was used as a hospital during the battle and Lieutenant-Colonel Monckton was buried in the cemetery. (Author's photograph)**

ready and nearer 8.00am when the last of them passed Lee on the road out of Englishtown. Some 660 men, including those too sick to march, were detailed to guard the baggage and the men's packs, which were to be left behind. Many men also left their coats and marched in shirtsleeves as it was already hot. Meanwhile, the same message from Dickinson had reached Washington at Manalapan Bridge and he ordered his own troops to move, before sending an order to Lee to "bring on an engagement or attack as soon as possible unless some very powerful circumstances forbid it." As Lee prepared to leave, another message arrived from Dickinson, stating that only one British division had left and another still remained, but as he rode toward Tennent Meetinghouse, one of von Steuben's aides insisted that the British had not left at all.

Behind Grayson, who had orders to halt and wait two miles outside Englishtown, the planned order of march was Varnum's Brigade (under Colonel John Durkee), Wayne's, Scott's, and Maxwell's, and finally a detachment of Continentals under Colonel Henry Jackson.

As a portent of the confusion that would mark the day, Maxwell (who had just been admonished by Lee for not having left already) set off only to find himself ahead of Wayne and Scott. Before reaching Tennent Meetinghouse, Maxwell received orders to turn south toward Craig's Mill, and halt at the first crossroad. Lee was still concerned that Clinton might outflank him via the Allentown road, and attack Englishtown. However, once it was clear that both British divisions were moving east, he ordered Maxwell to rejoin the column and posted two militia units in a farm on high ground next to the road instead.

On the Englishtown road, Dickinson's militia had made the first contact of the day around 7.30am. He had sent small parties of 10 or 12 militia to reconnoiter east of Tennent Meetinghouse and contacted the hussars and grenadiers of the Queen's Rangers (whose green coats led the militia to think they were jägers). Initially, the hussars scattered the militia, who fell back on their main body, which held the hussars at bay from behind a fence. The grenadiers then struck their left flank and forced them back to another position with more secure flanks. At that point, the Queen's Rangers saw a large enemy column approaching and withdrew toward Monmouth Courthouse.

That column was Grayson's detachment, which had now reached the Tennent Meetinghouse where the road dog-legged south then east. Halting his men half a mile past the church, Grayson rode forward to the bridge over Spotswood Middle Brook (often referred to during Lee's trial as the West Morass), where he met Dickinson. The latter asked Grayson to support his retreat and advised against any further advance as the bridge was the only way over the brook and Grayson would be trapped with the marsh at his back, especially if other British units outflanked him to the north. As Dickinson spoke, Lee and Wayne arrived and he repeated the warning to them.

Despite receiving constant (and conflicting) reports from all and sundry, Lee was convinced that Clinton intended to continue his march and any troops remaining at Monmouth Courthouse were a rearguard. Ordering Grayson to proceed with caution, he sent Jackson to join him at the front of the column and asked Wayne to take charge of those two detachments and a third unit (taken from Scott's command) under fellow Pennsylvanian Colonel Richard Butler.

Brigadier General Louis Lebeque de Presle Du Portail (1743–1802) by C.W. Peale. Du Portail entered the French army in 1765 and was a lieutenant colonel of engineers ten years later. One of several French officers given indefinite leave to serve in America, he is known today as the father of the US Army Corps of Engineers. (Independence National Historical Park)

View east from the Wikoff (West Rhea) Farm. The field on the left marks one of Oswald's battery positions during the retreat. The woods in the distance (which were not there in 1778, nor the road in the foreground) mark the direction from which the two British Grenadier battalions and the left wing of the 16th Light Dragoons were attacking. (Author's photograph)

Led by these three detachments and four guns under Lieutenant Colonel Eleazar Oswald of the 2nd Continental Artillery, Lee's division began crossing the bridge, only to be halted by reports of unidentified troops to the north, just as Dickinson had warned. They were eventually identified as local militia, but only after Scott and Durkee had re-crossed to the west side of the bridge. The delay meant that it was almost 9.00am before the division was under way again, with Maxwell's Brigade now in the rear.

Lee attacks

Clinton's army had spent an uneventful night at Freehold. He still believed that Washington's primary objective was the baggage train rather than a full-scale battle, as the main American army was reported six miles to Lee's rear – much too far away to support a major attack. Around 4.00am (an hour later than planned) Knyphausen's division began its 16-mile march to Middletown. The column, almost ten miles long, included all the Hessian troops except the Grenadiers, all of the Loyalist units, and the British 1st and 2nd Brigades who were guarding the wagons. The Jäger Korps brought up the rear, and to the north, the vulnerable left flank was covered by the 17th Light Dragoons, the 2nd Light Infantry, and the veteran 40th Foot.

Knyphausen had marched several miles through close, wooded country when, around noon, a handful of militia slipped past the flank guards. They attacked the baggage train, wounding two or three men and as many horses, before being driven off by the 17th Light Dragoons and some jägers. Another group of 50 militia then approached the wagons, but withdrew when approached by two companies of the 40th Foot. As still more militia appeared, the 10th and 49th Foot, guarding the flank of the artillery park, were sent to the rear of the column with a pair of 3-pdrs. The remainder of Grant's 2nd Brigade later joined them, but no further attacks materialized.

Clinton had spent the previous day scouting the surrounding countryside and considered it favorable for defense. Around 8.00am, confident that he no longer faced any serious threat, he ordered Cornwallis to prepare to leave. Shortly before 10.00am, the British 3rd, 4th, and 5th Brigades moved out, followed by the Foot Guards, the Hessian Grenadiers, and finally the British Grenadiers. Clinton remained with the rearguard (1,300 men from the 16th Light Dragoons, 1st Light Infantry, and Queen's Rangers) posted behind a ravine that contained Spotswood

Middle Brook (later referred to in Lee's trial as the East Morass). The ravine ran from the open fields north of Monmouth Courthouse, past thick woods near the junction with the road to Forman's Mills, increasing in depth as it did so. In contrast to Clinton, Lee knew nothing of the ravine. When informed of it later that morning, he merely replied that troops would have to make the best of it.

At about 9.30am, as the leading troops of Lee's division passed through a narrow defile and moved up the hill toward Monmouth Courthouse, British horsemen were seen to the south. Lee and Wayne crossed Spotswood Middle Brook and observed around 600 light cavalry and infantry, which they assumed was the entire British rearguard. Lee ordered Wayne to take Butler's and Jackson's detachments and drive back the enemy skirmishers, whilst Grayson held the junction with the road leading to Forman's Mills. The Continentals exchanged shots with the Queen's Rangers infantry, whom they forced back into an orchard near the courthouse. Wayne's units then came under well-aimed artillery fire and fell back into the woods in their rear, leaving two of Oswald's guns, which had pushed through some woods on Wayne's left flank, alone in the open.

At that point Lee halted his division and rode forward with Wayne to observe the enemy. Spotting the clouds of dust thrown up by Cornwallis's division heading for Middletown, Lee saw an opportunity to "pin" Clinton's rearguard (now moving east from the courthouse) whilst the rest of his division swept around their left to encircle them. Sending his aide, Captain John Mercer, to tell Wayne to press the enemy only enough to prevent them from falling back on their main body or receiving any reinforcements, he ordered Grayson's detachment to rejoin Butler and Jackson as the latter swung around to the north.

As Wayne advanced, he learned that, because of their police role in Philadelphia (and despite bringing an ammunition convoy with them when they rejoined the army), Jackson's men had just 12 rounds apiece. After a delay whilst Jackson's sergeants collected one round from every soldier in the other two detachments, Butler advanced covered by a party of militia horse under Lieutenant Colonel Anthony White. Passing through a cider orchard, Butler, followed by Jackson, entered an open plain northeast of the village. His men were hidden long enough for a party of British cavalry to believe that the militia horsemen were alone, and they charged the American horsemen, who fell back. As they did so, Butler's detachment emerged from the trees, formed line and gave the British dragoons a volley; Jackson's men appeared at the same time, but held their fire. The cavalry halted about 40 yards away and fired their pistols before riding off, disordering the dismounted dragoons supporting

View west from the Craig Farm. The farm was used as a hospital during the battle and British troops were rumored to have found the family's silver in a nearby well. Grey's 3rd Brigade came through the trees on the far left just after noon in pursuit of Scott's detachments. Perrine Ridge can be seen in the far distance to the left of the farmhouse. (Author's photograph)

them. As Butler and Jackson followed, they were fired on by a pair of 3-pdrs accompanying the 1st Light Infantry and forced to take cover in a wood to their left rear. During the action, Lee had mistaken Butler's and Jackson's detachments for the enemy and had deployed Durkee to attack them. The mistake was discovered in time and Durkee went to support Oswald's battery instead, but was wounded soon after and command of his detachment devolved on Lieutenant Colonel Jeremiah Olney.

Lee retreats

It was now around 10.00am, and Lee's main body (Wayne's command – now under La Fayette – followed by Scott, then Maxwell) was arriving, producing large clouds of dust that must have removed any element of surprise. Lee briefly contemplated anchoring his right flank on the village around Monmouth Courthouse, but abandoned the idea on learning that the buildings were made of wood, rather than stone, and too widely dispersed for interlocking fire. Instead, La Fayette was ordered to enter the plain northeast of the village, wheel left, and attack the left flank of Clinton's rearguard with the detachments of Colonels Walter Stewart, Henry Livingston, and James Wesson (some 800 men), and Captain Thomas Seward's two guns. The brigade formed up some 600 yards (546m) from the British line, with Stewart on the right, Wesson on the left, and Livingston in the center. As they advanced, they immediately came under artillery fire that caused a number of casualties including Wesson, who was replaced by Lieutenant Colonel Nathaniel Ramsay.

At the same time, Lee sent an aide to look for the rest of his division. Such were Lee's expectations of success that he had apparently indicated to both Dr James McHenry, Washington's Secretary, and La Fayette that he expected to capture the entire rearguard. However, unknown to him, the tables were about to be turned.

Clinton responds

The British commander in chief still believed that the enemy's objective was to attack his baggage train, and so he decided to force the Americans to halt their efforts by charging the troops in front of his rearguard with as many men as he could muster. Because of the heat, Cornwallis's division had not marched very far, and when he received Clinton's order to return, he was barely a mile north of where the Middletown and Shrewsbury roads met, near to where it was joined by a small track leading north to Scots Meetinghouse. As Clinton arrived at the junction of the Middletown and Shrewsbury roads, he immediately saw how vulnerable Lee's right was and decided to turn it. He ordered the Queen's Rangers and 1st Light Infantry to tie down Wayne, and then formed Cornwallis's

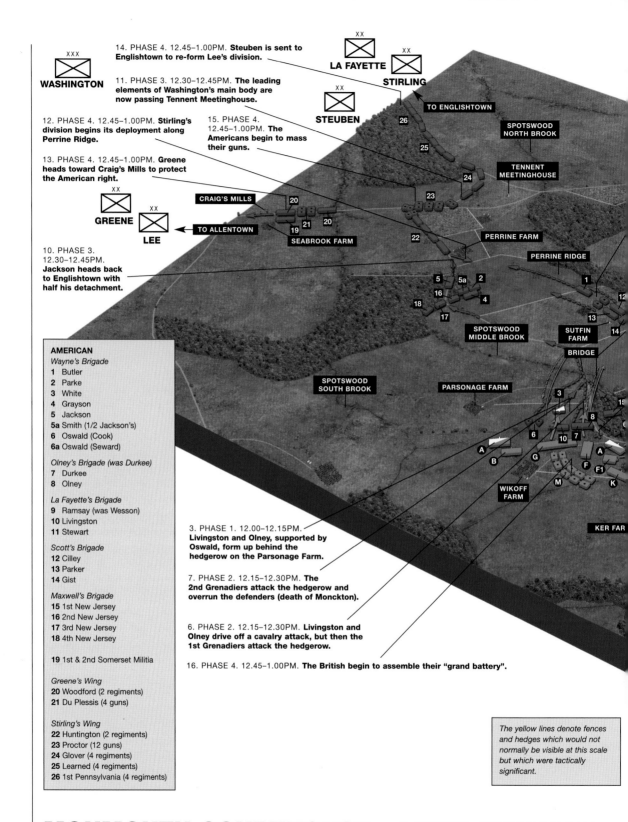

14. PHASE 4. 12.45–1.00PM. **Steuben is sent to Englishtown to re-form Lee's division.**

11. PHASE 3. 12.30–12.45PM. **The leading elements of Washington's main body are now passing Tennent Meetinghouse.**

12. PHASE 4. 12.45–1.00PM. **Stirling's division begins its deployment along Perrine Ridge.**

15. PHASE 4. 12.45–1.00PM. **The Americans begin to mass their guns.**

13. PHASE 4. 12.45–1.00PM. **Greene heads toward Craig's Mills to protect the American right.**

10. PHASE 3. 12.30–12.45PM. **Jackson heads back to Englishtown with half his detachment.**

WASHINGTON

LA FAYETTE

STIRLING

STEUBEN

GREENE

LEE

CRAIG'S MILLS

TO ALLENTOWN

SEABROOK FARM

TO ENGLISHTOWN

SPOTSWOOD NORTH BROOK

TENNENT MEETINGHOUSE

PERRINE FARM

PERRINE RIDGE

SPOTSWOOD MIDDLE BROOK

SUTFIN FARM

BRIDGE

SPOTSWOOD SOUTH BROOK

PARSONAGE FARM

WIKOFF FARM

KER FAR

AMERICAN

Wayne's Brigade
1 Butler
2 Parke
3 White
4 Grayson
5 Jackson
5a Smith (1/2 Jackson's)
6 Oswald (Cook)
6a Oswald (Seward)

Olney's Brigade (was Durkee)
7 Durkee
8 Olney

La Fayette's Brigade
9 Ramsay (was Wesson)
10 Livingston
11 Stewart

Scott's Brigade
12 Cilley
13 Parker
14 Gist

Maxwell's Brigade
15 1st New Jersey
16 2nd New Jersey
17 3rd New Jersey
18 4th New Jersey

19 1st & 2nd Somerset Militia

Greene's Wing
20 Woodford (2 regiments)
21 Du Plessis (4 guns)

Stirling's Wing
22 Huntington (2 regiments)
23 Proctor (12 guns)
24 Glover (4 regiments)
25 Learned (4 regiments)
26 1st Pennsylvania (4 regiments)

3. PHASE 1. 12.00–12.15PM. **Livingston and Olney, supported by Oswald, form up behind the hedgerow on the Parsonage Farm.**

7. PHASE 2. 12.15–12.30PM. **The 2nd Grenadiers attack the hedgerow and overrun the defenders (death of Monckton).**

6. PHASE 2. 12.15–12.30PM. **Livingston and Olney drive off a cavalry attack, but then the 1st Grenadiers attack the hedgerow.**

16. PHASE 4. 12.45–1.00PM. **The British begin to assemble their "grand battery".**

The yellow lines denote fences and hedges which would not normally be visible at this scale but which were tactically significant.

MONMOUTH COURTHOUSE – LEE'S RETREAT

Sunday, 28 June 1778, 12.00–1.00pm, viewed from the southeast, showing the retreat of Lee's Division and Washington's main body deploying.

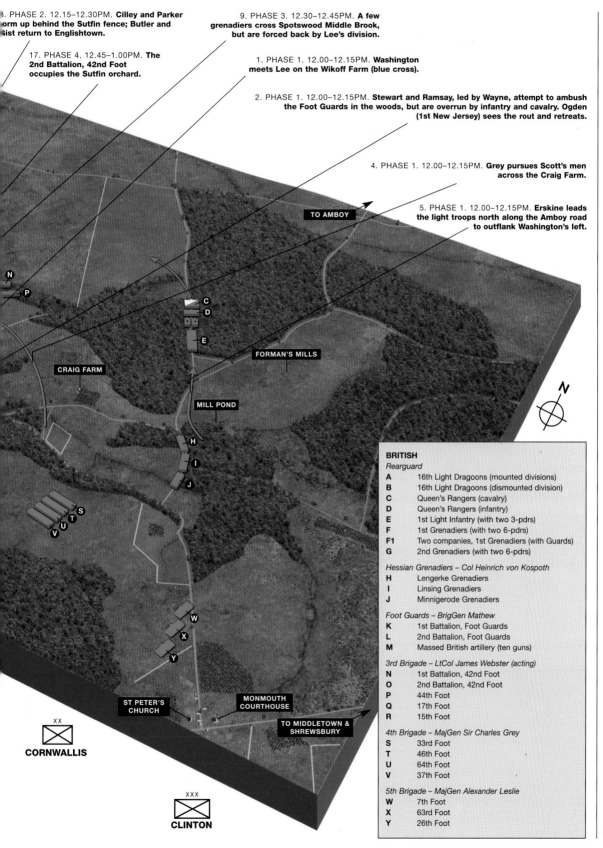

3. PHASE 2. 12.15–12.30PM. Cilley and Parker
·orm up behind the Sutfin fence; Butler and
·ist return to Englishtown.

9. PHASE 3. 12.30–12.45PM. A few
grenadiers cross Spotswood Middle Brook,
but are forced back by Lee's division.

17. PHASE 4. 12.45–1.00PM. The
2nd Battalion, 42nd Foot
occupies the Sutfin orchard.

1. PHASE 1. 12.00–12.15PM. Washington
meets Lee on the Wikoff Farm (blue cross).

2. PHASE 1. 12.00–12.15PM. Stewart and Ramsay, led by Wayne, attempt to ambush
the Foot Guards in the woods, but are overrun by infantry and cavalry. Ogden
(1st New Jersey) sees the rout and retreats.

4. PHASE 1. 12.00–12.15PM. Grey pursues Scott's men
across the Craig Farm.

TO AMBOY

5. PHASE 1. 12.00–12.15PM. Erskine leads
the light troops north along the Amboy road
to outflank Washington's left.

N
P

C
D

E

FORMAN'S MILLS

CRAIG FARM

MILL POND

H

I

J

S
T
U
V

W

X

Y

ST PETER'S
CHURCH

MONMOUTH
COURTHOUSE

TO MIDDLETOWN &
SHREWSBURY

xx
CORNWALLIS

xxx
CLINTON

BRITISH	
Rearguard	
A	16th Light Dragoons (mounted divisions)
B	16th Light Dragoons (dismounted division)
C	Queen's Rangers (cavalry)
D	Queen's Rangers (infantry)
E	1st Light Infantry (with two 3-pdrs)
F	1st Grenadiers (with two 6-pdrs)
F1	Two companies, 1st Grenadiers (with Guards)
G	2nd Grenadiers (with two 6-pdrs)
Hessian Grenadiers – Col Heinrich von Kospoth	
H	Lengerke Grenadiers
I	Linsing Grenadiers
J	Minnigerode Grenadiers
Foot Guards – BrigGen Mathew	
K	1st Battalion, Foot Guards
L	2nd Battalion, Foot Guards
M	Massed British artillery (ten guns)
3rd Brigade – LtCol James Webster (acting)	
N	1st Battalion, 42nd Foot
O	2nd Battalion, 42nd Foot
P	44th Foot
Q	17th Foot
R	15th Foot
4th Brigade – MajGen Sir Charles Grey	
S	33rd Foot
T	46th Foot
U	64th Foot
V	37th Foot
5th Brigade – MajGen Alexander Leslie	
W	7th Foot
X	63rd Foot
Y	26th Foot

division into two columns with his artillery in the middle and the cavalry covering the front. Leaving the lethargic Hessian Grenadiers in reserve, he launched his right-hand column at Lee's center and the other column towards the courthouse.

As Lee once again reconnoitered the British lines, he now saw not 600 men, but ten times that number – exceeding his own force – forming up on high ground a mile away. The situation was clearly reversed, with Lee's division now in danger of being surrounded. He doubted that the Continentals were up to facing Clinton's best troops, but with his plan nullified and no sign of Morgan providing any kind of diversion to the south, he had no choice.

As he rode along his line to find a better observation point, he saw Oswald taking his two guns to the rear, and demanded to know why. Oswald explained that the eastward shift of Butler's and Jackson's detachments had left his guns completely isolated. Moreover, one piece was now disabled with two men and two horses dead and the remaining gunners suffering from fatigue, whilst his ammunition wagon had been unable to cross the ravine and he had no more roundshot. Lee immediately gave him permission to continue to the rear and sent Captain John Mercer, and then later Captain Evan Edwards, to find Scott and order him to hold his ground.

Unfortunately, Scott had also seen the British columns. Somewhere around 10.30am, he had led his command over Spotswood North Brook into the orchard recently vacated by Butler and Jackson. Leaving Colonel Joseph Cilley to form up the brigade, he had ridden forward to reconnoiter the enemy, during which it is likely that he met and conferred with Wayne. Concerned that he would be cut off, Scott had then ridden back to his brigade to find someone to give him further orders. On the track behind the orchard, he found Maxwell and his New Jersey brigade and, as the two men conferred, Lee's adjutant, Lieutenant Colonel John Brooks, appeared. Asked if he had any new orders, Brooks replied that he did not, at which Scott and Maxwell decided to retreat as the troops to their right and left appeared to be pulling back (at that precise moment, only Oswald's gunners were actually withdrawing, but Scott may also have seen Butler and Jackson falling back into the woods northeast of the cider orchard).

Scott then fell back across Spotswood Middle Brook into some thick woods, and re-formed his brigade at 90 degrees to establish a line facing, rather than flanking, the approaching British columns (unfortunately these woods screened Scott's Brigade so effectively that Lee's aides could not find him). At the same time, Maxwell took the two heaviest of Scott's six guns and led his brigade back to the Amboy road, and then around onto the Englishtown road, in an attempt to extend Scott's line southward to Monmouth Courthouse and link up with La Fayette.

Meanwhile, in attempting to find Scott, Mercer had met Jackson, (who had also just seen Oswald withdrawing and had sent his second-in-command, Lieutenant Colonel William Smith, to obtain new orders). Jackson wanted to withdraw and had already declined an earlier invitation from Grayson to attack the right wing of the British rearguard on the high ground north of the junction of the Middletown and Shrewsbury roads. Mercer advised Jackson to stay where he was and rode off to look for Scott; he returned minutes later to find Jackson pulling

Lieutenant Colonel Nathaniel Ramsay (1741–1817) by R. Peale. A lawyer and one of Maryland's delegates to the Continental Congress, Ramsay had been an officer in Smallwood's Maryland Regiment during its vital rearguard action on Long Island, in 1776. His role in checking the British pursuit on 28 June was almost as important. (Independence National Historical Park)

View east from Spotswood Middle Brook. This was roughly the view Ogden and the 1st New Jersey had of the defeat of Stewart and Ramsay (the main road now follows a different line and in 1778 was closer to the dead tree in the left foreground). Olney and Livingston were posted to the right, on the rising ground by the lone tree. (Author's photograph)

back across the ravine, and ordered Grayson to do the same. At the same time, Butler – whom Mercer had also seen, but had not spoken to – found himself hemmed in on three sides and on lower ground than the advancing British columns. He had sent Major Benjamin Ledyard of the 1st New York Regiment to learn where the rest of Lee's division had gone, but before Ledyard returned, Butler was forced to fall back across Spotswood North Brook and circle to the north of Forman's Mills on the Amboy road. Mercer then met Edwards and they both rode back to tell Lee they could not find Scott, only to find that Brooks had already informed Lee of his meeting with Scott and Maxwell. With over 3,000 men and all ten of his guns leaving the field without orders, an angry Lee saw no option but to order a general retreat.

East of the courthouse, La Fayette received a message from Lee that Scott had withdrawn (he later claimed that Lee also told him to fall back, but neither Lee nor any other officer recalled either issuing or delivering such an order). La Fayette immediately withdrew all three regiments to an orchard near the courthouse, but the British advance split the brigade, leaving La Fayette with only Livingston's detachment still under command, and no option but to fall back himself. Less than ten minutes after reporting Scott's withdrawal to Lee, Mercer saw La Fayette falling back on the right, toward the courthouse. Lee also observed this movement, and remarked that this was another withdrawal without orders, but that at least this retreat solved a problem rather than causing one. Giving instructions for all units to rendezvous at their original position, north of Monmouth Courthouse, Lee rode back across the Great Ravine. It was approximately 11.30am.

Lee's entire division was now streaming back towards Tennent Meetinghouse. Maxwell, Jackson, Grayson, and La Fayette were on or south of the Englishtown road, covered by Oswald, who had assembled a "grand battery" of ten guns. Scott was withdrawing up the Amboy road and Butler was near the pond at Forman's Mills (Ledyard had by now returned with news that everyone was retreating, at which Butler had decided to continue heading east, across the Craig Farm). As the Americans began to regroup, Wayne apparently received a message from Morgan, three miles to the south at Richmond's Mills, asking for orders. Wayne pointed out, somewhat sarcastically, that since Lee's division was falling back and the enemy advancing, Morgan should "govern himself accordingly." Unfortunately, Wayne not only declined to advise Morgan himself, he also

THE CAPTURE OF LIEUTENANT COLONEL RAMSAY
(pages 54–55)

Just after noon, Washington removed Lee from his command, and then set about delaying the British long enough to establish his main defensive line, west of the bridge across Spotswood Middle Brook. The first units that he turned to were the detachments of "picked men" (1) commanded by Colonel Walter Stewart of Pennsylvania and Lieutenant Colonel Nathaniel Ramsay (2) of Maryland. In fact, Ramsay had been in command of his battalion for less than an hour, having replaced Colonel James Wesson when the latter was wounded during La Fayette's advance east of Monmouth Courthouse. Both Stewart and Ramsay agreed to stand and face the northernmost of the two British columns advancing from Monmouth Courthouse. Unknown to them, it was led by the Composite Brigade of Foot Guards – one of the best units in Clinton's army. The two units occupied a dense wood that encompassed the main road from Englishtown to Monmouth Courthouse – later referred to in Lee's trial as "point of woods" – with Ramsay to the left of Stewart (i.e. farther from the bridge). As the British column passed their position, Wayne ordered both units to open fire. The volley took the Foot Guards by surprise, and may have caused some loss, as they later reported over 40 combat casualties (including the

commander of the leading battalion) despite seeing no other action during the day. However, the firing did not halt the redcoats and they wheeled right and charged into the wood. Despite some hand-to-hand fighting, the issue seems to have been decided quite quickly and both detachments were forced out of the wood and back across the open ground toward the bridge (3) – their only line of escape. Once in the open, they were attacked by several troopers of the 16th Light Dragoons (4). Stewart was injured early on, and was carried from the field by his men (5). However, Ramsay's unit, being farther from the bridge, took the brunt of the assault and appears to have broken up into small groups. Whilst Ramsay attempted to rally his men, his horse was wounded and he found himself on foot. Almost immediately, a dragoon rode up and tried to shoot him with a pistol, but the weapon misfired. The trooper then drew his saber, but Ramsay wounded the man with his sword and then took the redcoat's horse. A party of dragoons then surrounded him and, during the ensuing swordfight, he was wounded so severely that he was initially left for dead and only taken prisoner later in the day. The following day, Clinton heard of Ramsay's bravery and immediately paroled him and had him escorted back to the American lines, although he was not officially exchanged until December 1780. (Adam Hook)

Washington replaces Lee, by Emmanuel Leutze. Painted not long after the discovery of the plan Lee had prepared for Howe, this work displays all the dramatic and righteous indignation one might expect from a betrayed Washington, and the sullen silence of an embarrassed Lee. Whilst the uniform details are good, Washington was still riding a white horse at this stage, and neither La Fayette nor Hamilton (to Washington's right) were with him. (Monmouth County Historical Association)

failed to pass the communication to Lee, who remained ignorant of Morgan's position all day. This omission lost Lee a valuable opportunity to relieve the pressure on his division via an attack against Clinton's vulnerable left rear.

By now desperate to find a defensible position, Lee asked the French engineer officer, Brigadier General Lebeque du Portail, to reconnoiter the ground to the immediate rear. The Frenchman discovered some high ground around a small farm rented by a Mr Ker (sometimes referred to as the East Rhea Farm) and Lee attempted to rally his division there. Despite some initial confusion and the close proximity of Clinton's cavalry, the withdrawal was orderly, the men moving at the double across the fields with Lee himself urging them on. Stewart and Livingston attempted to form a line based on the farm, but were soon forced to fall back as the advancing British columns looked like isolating them. As Stewart withdrew, his unit was threatened by British cavalry and turned to face them, but they fell back to the safety of their own infantry and Stewart's men continued their withdrawal.

When Lee reached the Ker Farm, he saw that higher ground to the east of the rise on which the farm stood made the position untenable. As Oswald prepared to fall back once more, he received orders from Lee to hold his position; almost immediately one of La Fayette's aides arrived with orders for him to withdraw. Luckily the officer persuaded Oswald that this second order came from Lee and countermanded the earlier one, and led Oswald back to a new position where the "grand battery" was dispersed. The guns belonging to Olney's detachment and Maxwell's Brigade were returned to their parent units, whilst Wells' two guns were sent back to Englishtown, the crews barely able to stand from exhaustion.

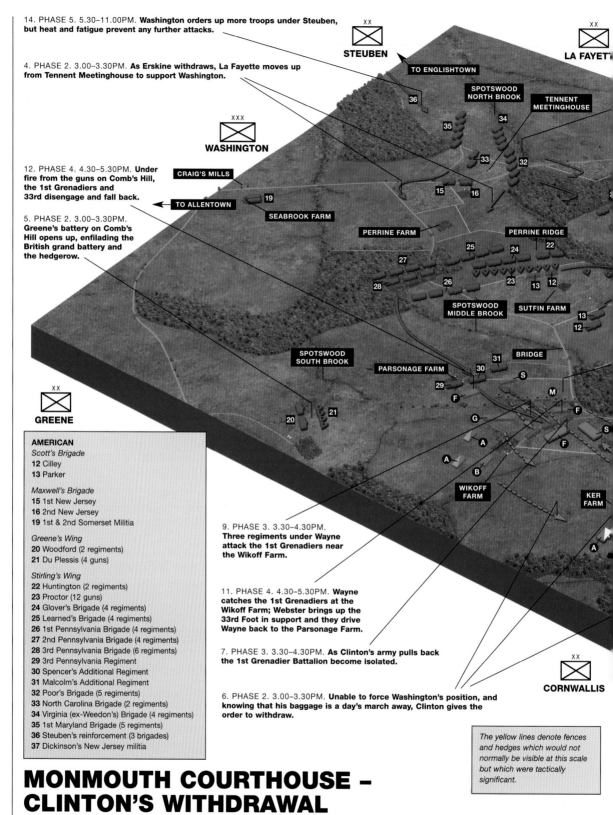

14. PHASE 5. 5.30–11.00PM. **Washington orders up more troops under Steuben, but heat and fatigue prevent any further attacks.**

STEUBEN

LA FAYETT

TO ENGLISHTOWN

SPOTSWOOD
NORTH BROOK

TENNENT
MEETINGHOUSE

4. PHASE 2. 3.00–3.30PM. **As Erskine withdraws, La Fayette moves up from Tennent Meetinghouse to support Washington.**

36

34

35

WASHINGTON

33   32

12. PHASE 4. 4.30–5.30PM. **Under fire from the guns on Comb's Hill, the 1st Grenadiers and 33rd disengage and fall back.**

CRAIG'S MILLS

15   16

TO ALLENTOWN

19

SEABROOK FARM

PERRINE FARM

PERRINE RIDGE

5. PHASE 2. 3.00–3.30PM. **Greene's battery on Comb's Hill opens up, enfilading the British grand battery and the hedgerow.**

25   24   22

27

23   13   12

28

26

SPOTSWOOD
MIDDLE BROOK

SUTFIN FARM

13

12

SPOTSWOOD
SOUTH BROOK

31

BRIDGE

PARSONAGE FARM

30

S

GREENE

29

F

20   21

G

M

F

A

S

A

F

A

B

AMERICAN
Scott's Brigade
12 Cilley
13 Parker

WIKOFF
FARM

KER
FARM

Maxwell's Brigade
15 1st New Jersey
16 2nd New Jersey
19 1st & 2nd Somerset Militia

A

9. PHASE 3. 3.30–4.30PM. **Three regiments under Wayne attack the 1st Grenadiers near the Wikoff Farm.**

Greene's Wing
20 Woodford (2 regiments)
21 Du Plessis (4 guns)

Stirling's Wing
22 Huntington (2 regiments)
23 Proctor (12 guns)
24 Glover's Brigade (4 regiments)
25 Learned's Brigade (4 regiments)
26 1st Pennsylvania Brigade (4 regiments)
27 2nd Pennsylvania Brigade (4 regiments)
28 3rd Pennsylvania Brigade (6 regiments)
29 3rd Pennsylvania Regiment
30 Spencer's Additional Regiment
31 Malcolm's Additional Regiment
32 Poor's Brigade (5 regiments)
33 North Carolina Brigade (2 regiments)
34 Virginia (ex-Weedon's) Brigade (4 regiments)
35 1st Maryland Brigade (5 regiments)
36 Steuben's reinforcement (3 brigades)
37 Dickinson's New Jersey militia

11. PHASE 4. 4.30–5.30PM. **Wayne catches the 1st Grenadiers at the Wikoff Farm; Webster brings up the 33rd Foot in support and they drive Wayne back to the Parsonage Farm.**

7. PHASE 3. 3.30–4.30PM. **As Clinton's army pulls back the 1st Grenadier Battalion become isolated.**

CORNWALLIS

6. PHASE 2. 3.00–3.30PM. **Unable to force Washington's position, and knowing that his baggage is a day's march away, Clinton gives the order to withdraw.**

The yellow lines denote fences and hedges which would not normally be visible at this scale but which were tactically significant.

MONMOUTH COURTHOUSE – CLINTON'S WITHDRAWAL

Sunday, 28 June 1778, 1.00–11.00pm, viewed from the southeast. Clinton orders a withdrawal and despite Washington's efforts to disrupt this, he succeeds in disengaging in good order.

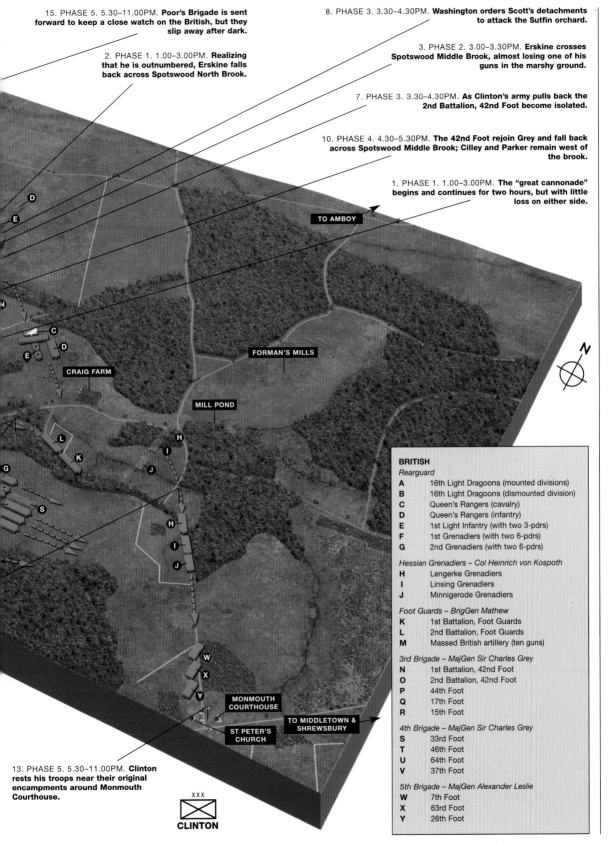

15. PHASE 5. 5.30–11.00PM. **Poor's Brigade is sent forward to keep a close watch on the British, but they slip away after dark.**

2. PHASE 1. 1.00–3.00PM. **Realizing that he is outnumbered, Erskine falls back across Spotswood North Brook.**

8. PHASE 3. 3.30–4.30PM. **Washington orders Scott's detachments to attack the Sutfin orchard.**

3. PHASE 2. 3.00–3.30PM. **Erskine crosses Spotswood Middle Brook, almost losing one of his guns in the marshy ground.**

7. PHASE 3. 3.30–4.30PM. **As Clinton's army pulls back the 2nd Battalion, 42nd Foot become isolated.**

10. PHASE 4. 4.30–5.30PM. **The 42nd Foot rejoin Grey and fall back across Spotswood Middle Brook; Cilley and Parker remain west of the brook.**

1. PHASE 1. 1.00–3.00PM. **The "great cannonade" begins and continues for two hours, but with little loss on either side.**

TO AMBOY

FORMAN'S MILLS

CRAIG FARM

MILL POND

MONMOUTH COURTHOUSE

TO MIDDLETOWN & SHREWSBURY

ST PETER'S CHURCH

13. PHASE 5. 5.30–11.00PM. **Clinton rests his troops near their original encampments around Monmouth Courthouse.**

XXX

CLINTON

BRITISH

Rearguard

A	16th Light Dragoons (mounted divisions)
B	16th Light Dragoons (dismounted division)
C	Queen's Rangers (cavalry)
D	Queen's Rangers (infantry)
E	1st Light Infantry (with two 3-pdrs)
F	1st Grenadiers (with two 6-pdrs)
G	2nd Grenadiers (with two 6-pdrs)

Hessian Grenadiers – Col Heinrich von Kospoth

H	Lengerke Grenadiers
I	Linsing Grenadiers
J	Minnigerode Grenadiers

Foot Guards – BrigGen Mathew

K	1st Battalion, Foot Guards
L	2nd Battalion, Foot Guards
M	Massed British artillery (ten guns)

3rd Brigade – MajGen Sir Charles Grey

N	1st Battalion, 42nd Foot
O	2nd Battalion, 42nd Foot
P	44th Foot
Q	17th Foot
R	15th Foot

4th Brigade – MajGen Sir Charles Grey

S	33rd Foot
T	46th Foot
U	64th Foot
V	37th Foot

5th Brigade – MajGen Alexander Leslie

W	7th Foot
X	63rd Foot
Y	26th Foot

As Lee was ordering another withdrawal, he met a local militia officer named Captain Peter Wikoff, who knew the area well and owned the West Rhea Farm. Lee explained that he needed ground that would support both flanks, and had plenty of shade for his men, who were dropping from fatigue. Wikoff advised that the nearest options – and those far from perfect – were either Comb's Hill to the southwest, or the ridge between Spotswood Middle Brook and the Tennent Meetinghouse. Lee rejected Comb's Hill, as his artillery could not cross the swampy ground in front of it. He sent Wikoff back toward Tennent with instructions to take the commander of the first unit he found to the other position, and to prevent any other corps from withdrawing beyond it. It was now about midday.

THE AFTERNOON ACTION

Whilst Lee and Wayne were reconnoitering the ground around Monmouth Courthouse earlier that morning, Washington's main body was passing through Englishtown, the men having discarded their packs, blankets, and in some cases even their coats. Around 11.00am, Washington sent Lee a verbal order to "annoy the enemy" but not let them "draw him into a scrape" before writing Congress that Lee's instructions were "to attack [the enemy's] rear if possible … before they get into strong grounds." As he left Englishtown, Washington met Hamilton, who informed him that Lee's division was about to meet Clinton's rearguard. They then rode to the head of the main column, now passing Tennent Meetinghouse, where a local man informed them that troops were retreating from the direction of Monmouth Courthouse. The man indicated a young fifer as the source of this information, and when Washington interviewed the youth he repeated his story. Despite threats to have him whipped the fifer persisted, at which he was put under guard to prevent him from spreading the story and causing panic among the troops.

By now, Washington was extremely concerned and sent ahead his secretary, Harrison, and an aide, Lieutenant Colonel John Fitzgerald, to obtain better intelligence. After crossing the bridge, Harrison met Colonel Matthias Ogden, commanding the 1st New Jersey Regiment, who up to that point had seen no action and felt that the retreat was unnecessary. As

View west toward Spotswood Middle Brook. A grenadier's view of the section of hedgerow defended by Olney. The road was much farther to the right in 1778 and the trees along the brook now mask Perrine Ridge. By all accounts the "west morass" was a considerable obstacle: Laurens called it an "impenetrable fen" and noted that it required much effort to get horses across; one Continental soldier recalled losing his shoes as he crossed it; and a doctor riding across the battlefield the next day found several dead men "mired to the waist." (Author's photograph)

OPPOSITE View east from Perrine Ridge. The Sutfin farmhouse is at the extreme right, the orchard was on the far left. The fence line defended by Cilley's and Parker's detachments during the "great cannonade" is clearly visible behind the nearest trees. Unfortunately it is no longer possible to see the position of the British battery (to the right of this view) due to the trees growing around Spotswood Middle Brook. (Author's photograph)

Harrison rode on he encountered Mercer, who announced that the British were close at hand, but still farther along the road he saw Maxwell, who also had no idea why he was retreating but was more concerned at the absence of any orders. Meanwhile, Fitzgerald had ridden almost as far as the Ker Farm and found Lee in a grain field, but almost at once some British dragoons forced them to withdraw.

Back at the bridge, Washington met Wikoff, who was following Lee's order to commandeer the first regiment he could find and lead it to the high ground between Spotswood Middle Brook and Tennent Meetinghouse. (This was the 2nd New Jersey, now Maxwell's lead regiment after he had posted Ogden and the 1st New Jersey in a wood just east of the bridge, as a rearguard.) The meeting was fortuitous since Washington knew nothing of the local terrain. After speaking to Wikoff, he ordered the rest of Maxwell's Brigade to occupy some woods to the south of Perrine Ridge and to rest and await further orders. Riding on, Washington met Grayson, who confirmed that Lee's entire division was retreating. Seeing how fatigued Grayson's men were, he ordered them to join Maxwell. At that moment several columns appeared and Washington rode forward to speak to Lee, who was at their head.

Washington takes charge

The meeting of Washington and Lee took place on the rising ground somwhere between the lane leading to the Wikoff Farm and the ditch dividing it from the Parsonage Farm. The most accurate accounts probably come from witness statements given at Lee's court-martial, most of which agree in the important aspects. The recollections of officers who were not there and were recalling events many years later, such as Scott (who famously quoted Washington cursing "till the leaves shook on the trees") and La Fayette (who had Washington calling Lee "a damned poltroon"), are unsupported by any eyewitness and remain highly suspect.

Lee's adjutant general, Brooks, recalled Washington asking why the troops were retreating and Lee replying that it was a combination of contradictory intelligence, and his [Lee's] orders not being obeyed. At this, Washington apparently became "warm" and remarked that Lee should not have requested the command if he had not intended to attack.

THE 42ND FOOT IN THE SUTFIN ORCHARD (pages 62–63)
Around 3.30pm, Washington observed the British force that
had been attempting to outflank his left (Erskine's light troops
and part of Grey's 3rd Brigade) withdrawing across Spotswood
North Brook and back towards the Englishtown road. The
withdrawal left the most forward British unit (in the Sutfin
apple orchard) exposed to attack from the north, and he
immediately ordered two battalions of "picked men" from
Scott's Brigade that had not returned to Englishtown to do just
that. These two units had been screening the front of
the artillery battery on Perrine Ridge following their hectic
withdrawal across the Craig Farm, and it took the senior
battalion commander, Colonel Joseph Cilley, some time to
round up his 400 men. He then led them into the trees
northwest of the orchard, over the ridge, and into the small
valley formed by Spotswood North Brook. He was followed
by another 250 men under Colonel Richard Parker, and two
cannon. Opposing them were approximately 320 men of the
2nd Battalion of the 42nd Foot (Royal Highland Regiment) – the
Black Watch (1) – who had marched 16 miles in under seven
hours, before spending the last two hours in the shelter of the
orchard. Concealed by the crest of the ridge, Cilley led his
men to within 200 yards of the north side of the orchard until
forced to break cover. Sheltering behind the apple trees, the
Highlanders suddenly spotted the threat and the right flank
company, under Captain Grant (2), formed up behind the rail

fence that surrounded the orchard. Unfortunately, this
exposed them to enfilading fire from one of the 6-pdrs
accompanying Parker, which caused some casualties (3).
Cilley and his second-in-command, Lieutenant Colonel Henry
Dearborn, then led their men forward in a two-rank line (4)
preceded by about 20 skirmishers (5) – including the diarist,
Joseph Plumb Martin. The 42nd withdrew in an orderly
fashion through the trees under a harassing fire from Cilley's
skirmishers (Martin recalled aiming between the shoulders
of one retreating redcoat) and re-formed in a field about
300 yards to the southeast. As Cilley's men emerged from the
orchard, the Highlanders fired a volley then fell back to the
northern edge of the morass around Spotswood Middle
Brook, where Erskine's rearguard was still crossing. Here the
42nd were supported by two 3-pdrs from the 1st Light
Infantry, firing case shot at the pursuing Americans. Several
volleys were exchanged (one of Cilley's men recalled firing
12 rounds in the entire action) before the 42nd withdrew
across the brook to rejoin their brigade. Cilley halted his men,
and then withdrew to the orchard. The action probably cost
the Highlanders three or four dead and perhaps eight
wounded. Cilley's loss is unknown as his men returned to
their regiments two days later; however, an examination of the
combat casualties of those 20 regiments (most of which were
not otherwise engaged) suggests twice the British figure.
(Adam Hook)

Major-General Sir Charles Grey (1729–1807) by James Watson. "No Flint" Grey had seen extensive service in the Seven Years War and was an acknowledged expert in the *petite guerre*, as Wayne had discovered at Paoli the previous year. (British Museum)

Lee then replied that in his opinion a major action was not in the best interests of the army (or possibly of America, Brooks could not recall which), adding that he had been perfectly willing to obey Washington's orders but that circumstances prevented it. Unsurprisingly perhaps, Mercer had similar recollections of the conversation. Dr James McHenry testified, however, that Washington twice asked Lee why he was retreating, mentioning that Lee's replies seemed confused and hesitant and Lee himself embarrassed (as Washington seldom shouted, it is possible that the noise of battle prevented Lee hearing the question).

Whatever the correct version, Washington relieved Lee of command and rode on, having learned from Harrison that the British were only 15 minutes' march away. As he did so, he met La Fayette (accompanied by Stewart and Ramsay), who gave a brief account of the day's events. Washington asked both colonels to hold the enemy up whilst he rode back and formed a defensive line; they agreed and halted their units on the road. At that moment, Wayne arrived and ordered both detachments into the woods beside the road, to ambush the nearer of the British columns.

Meanwhile, Lee had ridden back toward Tennent Meetinghouse and tried to halt Maxwell's men as they crossed the bridge. Mercer stopped him, however, explaining that since Washington had taken over his division Lee's orders might cause confusion. As Maxwell marched on, Lee rode back to Washington, who suggested that Lee take charge east of the bridge whilst a defensive line was organized. Lee agreed and Washington galloped back toward Perrine Ridge.

Lee sent an order to Jackson to form up behind a rail fence to check the British cavalry. Unfortunately, a civilian carried the order and not surprisingly Jackson ignored it, claiming his men were too tired (although Smith managed to form up half of the unit with little difficulty). When Lee learned of this he rode over and berated Jackson in person. At that point Jackson's wing then apparently heard an anonymous order: "Jackson, march on! March on!" and, leaving Smith's wing of the unit behind, retreated all the way to Englishtown without meeting another senior officer, or receiving any other orders.

An increasingly frustrated Lee then placed Olney's detachment behind a long hedgerow running approximately north–south, dividing the Wikoff and Parsonage farms. Two of Oswald's remaining four guns took post on a hill behind the hedgerow, supporting Olney along with the remaining militia horse. The other two guns covered Stewart and Ramsay. Livingston's detachment was then ordered to protect Oswald's right flank, but for some reason formed up in front, masking the guns. When Livingston was told to split his command either side of the battery he again failed to comply, this time moving his detachment to the left and behind the hedgerow, exposing Oswald's right once more.

At the same time Lee sent Mercer to the small wood at the north end of the hedgerow to make sure that the 1st New Jersey was ready to cover any retreat across the bridge – to the last man if necessary. Its commander, Colonel Ogden, replied that enemy troops (MajGen Sir Charles Grey's 3rd Brigade) had advanced across the fields to his left and were now behind him. Despite reassurances that he was in no more danger than anyone else, Ogden refused to agree to sacrifice his men.

Meanwhile, Wayne had finished deploying Stewart's and Ramsay's men, possibly augmented by a converged battalion of Virginians under

THE GUNS ON COMB'S HILL (pages 66–67)

Around noon, as Washington's main body had been passing Tennent Meetinghouse, he had sent Greene, with Woodford's Brigade and four guns, south toward the Allentown road to prevent Clinton from outflanking the American right. About an hour later, Washington sent Lieutenant Colonel David Rhea to find Greene and direct him to Comb's Hill, from where Greene could observe Clinton's army whilst protected on three sides by swamp (which Rhea assured him would require a four-mile detour to outflank). By 3.00pm, Greene had brought up a battery of four 6-pdrs commanded by a French nobleman, Chevalier Thomas-Antoine de Mauduit du Plessis (1), who was serving as plain Thomas Duplessis. He had recently been promoted to lieutenant colonel and was adjutant to Brigadier General Henry Knox, the overall commander of the Continental Army's artillery. However, he was also a talented graduate of the famous artillery school at Grenoble and had spent the spring of 1778 introducing Washington's officers to Guibert's *Essai General de Tactique*. Guibert stressed flexibility – infantry trained in both line and light tactics, and deploying in line or column (or even both, if required), supported directly by massed artillery firing at enemy infantry and cavalry – and such was the impact of Du Plessis's efforts that he had become as respected within the technical arms of service as Steuben was among the infantry. By 3.30pm, the battery was in action, firing into the left flank of the 2nd Grenadiers defending the hedgerow, and enfilading the British "grand battery" in front of it. So effective was this bombardment that

it appears to have been the final element in persuading Clinton to withdraw. Although the British fell back beyond the range of the battery, it later came to Wayne's rescue after the 1st Grenadiers and 33rd Foot (2) drove his troops (3) back to the Parsonage Farm around 5.30pm. As the British prepared to assault the farm buildings and orchard, the guns broke up their formations with roundshot and forced them to withdraw (according to legend, one shot struck the muskets from the hands of an entire platoon of grenadiers). Here a Corporal of the Continental Artillery (4) lays a brass 6-pdr on its target, squinting along the barrel to aim and making adjustments with the handspike in the gun's trail. The gunner with the rammer (5) has already rammed home the charge and shot and another gunner stands by with a powder horn (6) ready to prime the gun's touchhole, once it is correctly positioned. Only then will the fifth member of the gun's crew step forward with the linstock (7) to fire the piece. Several infantrymen (8) stand by to help the gunners manhandle the gun. The service of the guns on Comb's Hill typified the effort of the Continental Artillery throughout the day. Whilst Washington's infantry have invariably received the plaudits for putting into practice the lessons of Valley Forge, arguably it was the gunners – first under Oswald, then later under Knox and Du Plessis – who did most to deny Clinton victory. Afterwards, Washington said: "It is with particular pleasure that the commander in chief can inform General Knox and the officers of the artillery that the enemy have done them the justice to acknowledge that no artillery could be better served than ours." (Adam Hook)

Colonel James Woods[5], in the woods enclosing the Englishtown road. It may have been at this point that Mercer delivered an order from Lee for him to defend the woods as long as possible; on learning who the order was from, Wayne apparently rode away. The leading British units were barely 400 yards (364m) off, but Wayne believed they could be checked "provided any effort or exertion was made." As the leading battalion of the Foot Guards under Colonel Henry Trelawney drew level, Wayne ordered his troops to fire into their exposed flank. Despite losing about 40 men (including Trelawney, another officer and three sergeants) the Foot Guards and two companies of the 1st Grenadiers immediately counter-attacked. Both sides became hopelessly intermingled among the trees, but weight of numbers forced Stewart and Ramsay out of the woods and into the open ground leading to the bridge, where the 16th Light Dragoons took them in the flank. Stewart was injured and carried from the field. Ramsay was dismounted and slightly wounded, and was eventually captured after hand-to-hand combat with two enemy horsemen. Seeing the struggle in front of him, Ogden decided to retire. As Ogden and Wayne fell back across the morass, the Foot Guards and 1st Grenadiers re-formed behind the rail fence or sought shade and water in the scrub and woods around the bridge.

Moments later the action shifted to the Parsonage Farm, where an equally one-sided encounter was developing around the hedgerow. The initial assault was by the 16th Light Dragoons, who advanced to within 40 yards (37m) before they were driven off by musketry and decided to try to outflank the southern end of the hedgerow instead. However, checking the dragoons proved a short-lived success and the next assault was led by Clinton in person, shouting: "Charge, Grenadiers, never heed forming!" as the 2nd Grenadiers and the left wing of the 1st Grenadiers advanced in a jumble of companies. (Clinton was widely criticized for his personal involvement in the close fighting that typified the first half of the battle. At one stage, he had to be rescued by two of his staff when an American colonel tried to shoot him.)

Despite Oswald's guns firing grapeshot at a range of 40 yards (37m) through gaps in the fence, and a blaze of musketry at barely 20 yards

View north from Comb's Hill. The trees in the right foreground were not there in 1778 and obscure the site of the Parsonage Farm and hedgerow, which were clearly visible to the gunners. In the distance is Perrine Ridge, with the Sutfin farmhouse just right of center in the middle distance. (Author's photograph)

5 Originally part of Grayson's detachment.

(18m), the Grenadiers quickly overran the hedgerow. During the fighting, both Laurens and Hamilton had their horses shot from under them (since Brooks, de Malmedy, Mercer, and Edwards had also lost their mounts to fatigue or enemy fire, all of Lee's staff were now on foot as well). Within a few minutes, the situation became so desperate that Knox ordered Oswald to fall back over the bridge. With Ogden gone only Olney's men covered the withdrawal of Oswald's guns, and elements of the two Grenadier battalions chased them over the bridge. It was either at this point or in the initial charge against the hedgerow that Lieutenant-Colonel Henry Monckton was killed by grapeshot at the head of the 2nd Grenadiers. (Although at least one of his officers saw him fall and later sent men to reclaim the body, it was only recovered at the end of the day by men of the 1st Pennsylvania Regiment, which has since led to confusion over the time of his death.) In the confusion, four officers and a dozen grenadiers found themselves surrounded by Continentals. The latter were so intent on retreating, however, that they ignored the enemy, even though one British officer killed a private with his sword and the redcoats made at least one attempt to seize a regimental color (possibly from one of Olney's units).

Farther north, Scott's Brigade had crossed the fields of the Craig Farm, which lay between Spotswood Middle and North brooks. Scott had been followed by the 2nd Battalion, 42nd Foot, which had cut across Spotswood Middle Brook and followed him over the Sutfin Farm toward Perrine Ridge. The Highlanders were halted by artillery fire and fell back into a large orchard, where they were watched – and occasionally fired on – by Cilley's and Parker's detachments (Butler and Gist having gone on to Englishtown).

Everyone was now safely across the bridge over Spotswood Middle Brook without (as Lee later boasted) the loss of a gun, a color, or a battalion, and despite facing the best troops Clinton had, including a vastly superior force of cavalry. Lee rode over to Washington, possibly expecting thanks and praise. Instead, he was sent to reorganize his exhausted division which, except for the 1st and 2nd New Jersey, and Cilley's and Parker's detachments, had kept going toward Englishtown.

The defense of Perrine Ridge

On the east slope of Perrine Ridge, Washington and Stirling established a line composed of Huntington's, Glover's, Learned's, Conway's, and the 2nd Pennsylvania brigades. Screening their left front were Cilley's and

View west from the Sutfin Farm. The view Grey's Brigade had of the main American position: the dense treeline straight ahead marks the crest of Perrine Ridge. The large orchard occupied by the 2nd Battalion, 42nd Foot, was at the extreme right. Beyond the dense woods lies the valley of Spotswood North Brook (now McGeillard's Brook) that Cilley and Parker used to shield their attack on the orchard. (Author's photograph)

View southwest toward Weamacock Point. This is the approximate line of the British battery, in front of the hedgerow, and the ground over which Wayne retreated when counter-attacked by the 1st Grenadiers and 33rd Foot. Comb's Hill is to the left and the track runs along the western side of the hedgerow. The single large tree in the right middle distance marks the site of the Parsonage Farm. Perrine Ridge is away to the right, but is now obscured by the trees around Spotswood Middle Brook. (Author's photograph)

Parker's detachments, lining a fence half-way up the ridge (the boundary between the Perrine and Sutfin farms), while the right front was covered by the 1st Pennsylvania Brigade. Between 1.00pm and 1.30pm a large battery[6] was set up by Knox on the east slope of Perrine Ridge, just above the boundary fence.

Across the marshy valley, Clinton had assembled his artillery on the rise just west of the hedgerow. At a range of about 1,000 yards (910m), two medium 12-pdrs, two $5^1/2$in. howitzers, and six 6-pdrs returned the fire of Knox's 4- and 6-pdrs. Stirling immediately ordered his brigades to take cover in the woods and behind the ridge, and Clinton's infantry remained behind the hedgerow; nevertheless, the bombardment continued for more than two hours.

Meanwhile, Washington was having second thoughts about who should reorganize Lee's division and ordered Steuben to ride back, take command, and re-form it on the heights west of Englishtown. At the same time, La Fayette was told to establish a second line on high ground west of Tennent Meetinghouse, with Poor's, the North Carolina, the 1st Maryland, and Weedon's brigades and the 1st and 2nd New Jersey regiments. The Frenchman's role was to support Stirling and counter any British threat to the American left, north of Spotswood North Brook.

This threat appeared around 2.00pm, and involved part of Grey's 3rd Brigade (the 1st Battalion, 42nd Foot, and the 44th Foot), and elements of the rearguard under Erskine. Grey's men had chased Scott's detachments across the Craig Farm, before dropping their packs in a field and passing over Spotswood North Brook. They were joined by Erskine with the Queen's Rangers and 1st Light Infantry, supported by two 3-pdrs. They had let Cornwallis's division pass and then marched north up the Amboy road and over the Deacon John Craig Farm.

The two British contingents sparred for about an hour with Dickinson's militia and elements of La Fayette's second line, northeast of Tennent Meetinghouse, but it was soon clear that the enemy were too numerous. Around 3.00pm, Erskine (or possibly Clinton) ordered the troops back

---

6 Estimated by various observers at anything from ten to 14 guns, but most likely 12.

Major General Nathanael Greene (1742–86) by C.W. Peale. Greene had been reluctant to replace Thomas Mifflin as Quartermaster General, and insisted on retaining his field command as well. Nevertheless, he showed considerable skill in ensuring the Continental Army was properly supplied during its march across New Jersey. (Independence National Historical Park)

across Spotswood North Brook to rejoin the rest of Grey's 3rd Brigade east of the Sutfin Farm. During the withdrawal, one of the 3-pdrs became stuck in the marshy ground around Spotswood Middle Brook and may even have been captured briefly by the militia, before being rescued and dragged away by the Queen's Rangers.

The third phase: Clinton withdraws

Shortly after noon, Washington had ordered Greene to take Woodford's Brigade and four guns and march south from Tennent Meetinghouse toward the Allentown road, to forestall any British attempt to outflank him. However, soon afterward Washington had met Rhea, who had alerted him to the high ground overlooking the British left. Washington immediately sent Rhea to tell Greene of Lee's withdrawal across Spotswood Middle Brook and guide him onto Comb's Hill. Led by Rhea, Greene arrived at the summit of Comb's Hill around 3.00pm. From the summit Greene could see not only the extent of the British positions, but also that he was protected on three sides by the marshy valley of Spotswood South Brook. The elevation allowed the four guns commanded by Lieutenant Colonel Chevalier Antoine de Mauduit du Plessis to fire on the Foot Guards to the north of the Englishtown road, but more importantly they could enfilade the entire British line along the hedgerow, and the "grand battery" in front of it.

Clinton quickly spotted the danger from the guns on Comb's Hill and, with Erskine now falling back across the Craig Farm, he decided to order a general withdrawal. Seeing movement all along the British line, and having had the withdrawal confirmed by a staff officer, Washington decided to probe for weaknesses with a series of small, local counter-attacks. The first involved an attack against the Highlanders in the orchard by Scott's detachments on the forward slopes of Perrine Ridge. Cilley led his 350 men, followed by Parker with another 250, north through the trees along the top of Perrine Ridge and into the valley formed by Spotswood North Brook. This not only concealed him from the Highlanders in the orchard, but also allowed the guns on the forward slope of the Perrine Ridge to continue firing into the orchard. As Cilley came within 200 yards (182m) of the north side of the orchard, his men were spotted. The 42nd formed up along the rail fence around the orchard, but became exposed to enfilading fire from a 6-pdr brought forward to support Cilley's attack. The Highlanders fell back slowly through the orchard and into a low-lying meadow beside Spotswood Middle Brook, where they were hidden from the American guns. Cilley's men cleared the orchard, threw down a rail fence, and formed up to attack the 42nd, who were now supported by their own artillery (a pair of 3-pdrs). A brief exchange of volleys caused little loss on either side, and the Highlanders sensibly withdrew across Spotswood Middle Brook, leaving Cilley's men to take shelter from the heat and the 3-pdrs.

The second attack came south of the bridge. Encouraged by Cilley's apparent success, Wayne was ordered to probe the left flank of the British rearguard with three small regiments from the brigade formerly commanded by Conway – the 3rd Pennsylvania Regiment, and Malcolm's and Spencer's Additional regiments. Wayne emerged from the woods beside the Seabrook Farm and marched toward the British left, to discover that during their withdrawal the 1st Grenadiers had become isolated.

Wayne seized the opportunity and attacked, making contact just west of the Wikoff Farm, but the Grenadiers received a timely reinforcement. Lieutenant-Colonel James Webster, on his own initiative, had brought up the 33rd Foot, and the two units counter-attacked, driving Wayne's men back across the hedgerow. It was probably during this part of the fighting that Lieutenant Colonel Rudolph Bunner, commanding Spencer's Additional regiment, became the highest ranking American fatality of the day. Lieutenant Colonel Aaron Burr, leading Malcolm's Additional regiment, had his horse killed (both units also lost a number of rank-and-file). The fighting continued for some time and eventually the British forced Wayne's troops back into the Parsonage Farm. As the 1st Grenadiers followed, the guns on Comb's Hill again opened up and forced both British units to take cover to the north of the high ground around the hedgerow. They then fell back past the Wikoff and Ker farms to rejoin the rest of Clinton's force. By now Erskine and Grey had reached the Amboy road and, with all his units safe, Clinton rode back to Monmouth Courthouse.

As soon as Washington saw the last British units leaving the field, he ordered forward Poor's Brigade and the North Carolina Brigade, and gave them instructions to cross Spotswood Middle Brook and hit the British right. At the same time, Woodford's Virginians were to come down from Comb's Hill and strike just south of the Parsonage Farm. The assault was to be supported by artillery moving down from the heights east of the Tennent Meetinghouse and along the Englishtown road. Around the same time, Washington also ordered Steuben to bring more men forward. By now Steuben had finished reorganizing Lee's division and had been joined by Brigadier General John Patterson with three more brigades (his own, Muhlenberg's, and the 2nd Maryland, the last accompanied by a small artillery detachment), and it was these three formations that Steuben brought forward. By the time they arrived, however, it was past 6.00pm. The late hour, the heat, and the energy-sapping march across the dusty, undulating landscape, prevented even these relatively fresh units from catching the enemy. The attack was called off and Washington ordered his troops to sleep on the ground they occupied, in readiness for action first thing the next morning. In the meantime, he sent Poor's Brigade forward to within half a mile of the British outposts to warn him of any movement.

AFTERMATH

CLINTON REACHES SAFETY

Clinton rested his men only briefly before continuing his withdrawal, although accounts vary as to when the troops left Monmouth Courthouse – probably somewhere between 10.00pm and midnight. Despite American jibes that Clinton left "on tiptoe in the dark," the withdrawal was as rapid and effective as Washington's evasion of Cornwallis near Trenton 18 months earlier. Poor's Brigade, not half a mile away, heard nothing and by dawn next day Clinton and Cornwallis had joined Knyphausen at Nut Swamp, 13 miles (21km) away. Around 10.00am the entire force moved on to Middletown, where it remained until 30 June, when the 3rd, 4th, and 5th brigades, and Stirn's Hessians occupied the Heights of Navesink. By evening, they had been joined by the artillery park, the baggage train, and the rest of the army.

On 1 July, the embarkation of the baggage and stores began whilst a bridge of boats was constructed to span the 60-yard (55m) gap between the island on which the lighthouse stood and the mainland. On 5 July, despite heavy rain the army boarded the waiting transports: the 3rd, 4th, and 5th Brigades went to Long Island, the 1st and 2nd Brigades to Staten Island, and the Foot Guards, Hessians, and cavalry to York Island. It had taken Clinton's force less than two days to cover the last 24 miles (39km) to Sandy Hook, as opposed to nine days to cover the 60 miles (97km) from Philadelphia to Monmouth Courthouse (with just 40 miles covered in the first seven days). This has prompted suggestions that Clinton wanted Washington to catch him up.

Monmouth mythology. "Molly Pitcher" has been associated with almost every artillery formation that fought at Monmouth and the battlefield contains at least two "Molly Pitcher's wells". Mary Ludwig Hayes was the wife of a gunner in the 4th Continental Artillery, and on seeing her husband wounded (not killed) took his place in loading the cannon he was serving. She was probably the same woman that Joseph Plumb Martin saw lose her petticoat to a cannonball that passed between her legs, but it is unlikely (though not impossible) that she was introduced to Washington after the battle. (Monmouth County Historical Association)

More Monmouth mythology. According to legend, Lieutenant-Colonel Henry Monckton was killed in action against the 1st Pennsylvania Regiment at the end of the day, and both his corpse and his battalion's colors were captured. In fact, Monckton was killed around noon during the storming of the hedgerow (probably by grapeshot from Oswald's guns) and in any event his unit, being grenadiers, had no colors. The 1st Pennsylvania saw no fighting that day as a unit, although many of its personnel served in the battalions of "picked men". (Monmouth County Historical Association)

Both armies now took stock of their own losses, and played up those of their opponents. American estimates suggested that 440 Hessians and 136 British had deserted[7], in addition to over 100 prisoners taken during the ten days. In terms of the action of 28 June, Washington reported 362 casualties[8] but estimated Clinton's losses at over 2,000. An official British return dated 5 July gave their own casualties as 361 all ranks[9], including four wounded officers and 40 men left to Washington's care at Monmouth Courthouse. According to Clinton's secretary, Andrew Bell, the enemy had numbered 25,000 (a figure supposedly given by American deserters) from which Washington had lost 2,000 men, with both Lee and "a French general" among the dead.

Back at Englishtown, on 29 June, Washington conferred with his generals, who agreed that further pursuit was pointless, and he limited himself to ordering Maxwell and Morgan to round up deserters and to hinder British foraging parties. Maxwell's men were so fatigued they returned that evening, leaving the pursuit to Morgan and some light horse and rangers. Washington then issued a general order praising the army, and gave directions for disposing of the dead and treating the wounded. On 30 June, the enlistments of the New Jersey militia expired and they went home, whilst the Continentals rested, cleaned themselves and their equipment, and held a service of thanksgiving.

On 1 July, the army began its march back to New York City, leaving Englishtown around 2.00am. The heat forced them to make camp at

Lieutenant Colonel John Laurens (1754–82) by C.W. Peale. Son of Henry Laurens, president of the Continental Congress, he was educated in London and Geneva and returned to America in 1777, serving Washington as a volunteer aide and translator. He reconnoitered the British camp with Steuben on 27 June, and had his horse killed under him during the battle. Long before Lee's dealings with Howe were known, Laurens and his father both discussed the possibility of treachery on Lee's part. On 23 December 1778, he wounded Lee in a duel over comments by the latter about Washington. (Independence National Historical Park)

---

7 Knyphausen, in an official report, acknowledged 236 desertions. Returns for May and July show Hessian numbers fell by 400 (405 by overall strength, 402 for "fit and present"), including 23 battle casualties (1 killed, 11 dead from fatigue, 11 wounded – all combat losses falling on the Jäger Korps). In contrast, the seldom quoted figure for Continental desertions from January to June 1778 is over 1,500.

8 Eight officers and 61 enlisted men killed (including eight gunners), 19 officers and 142 enlisted men wounded; 132 enlisted men missing. Most of the missing came in soon afterward, according to Washington, a view partially supported by the "sick absent" figure in his June return – 5,066 against 1,670 at the end of May.

9 Four officers and 63 enlisted men killed, 59 enlisted men dead of fatigue; 15 officers and 155 enlisted men wounded; 65 enlisted men missing. These figures are disputed, based on Washington's claim of burying 245 British corpses, in addition to those supposedly buried by the British themselves, and those bodies being found daily in the woods by the local population. Unfortunately, British returns for July (showing 262 fewer enlisted men overall, but 556 fewer "fit and present for duty") are distorted by the numbers of "sick" and those listed "absent", which includes men on other duties.

Spotswood, just three miles away, however. Early the next morning, they marched to New Brunswick and camped either side of the Raritan River where they remained until 4 July. Two days later, Maxwell's Brigade went into quarters at Elizabethtown, whilst the other detached corps rejoined the main body. Marching through Scotch Plains and Paramus, the army camped at Haverstraw on 14 July. It then pushed on to King's Ferry, crossing the Hudson River three days later. On 24 July, Washington reached White Plains, where he was reinforced by Gates and began an investment of New York City that would last until the end of the war.

HOWE AGAINST D'ESTAING

The Comte d'Estaing had left Toulon in April with 12 ships of the line and five frigates, and orders to blockade the Delaware River. Not until 5 June did the British Admiralty realize that his destination was America and four days later a squadron under Vice Admiral the Honourable John Byron was sent to reinforce Howe. As it turned out, Byron did not reach New York City until 18 August and that Howe survived unaided for two months was down to a combination of his own resourcefulness and d'Estaing's errors.

Anticipating the evacuation of Philadelphia, Howe had brought every available warship from Newport and New York City to protect the transports. As Clinton left Philadelphia the fleet headed down the Delaware, but headwinds, calms, and natural obstacles meant that it did not reach the Atlantic until 28 June, and Sandy Hook two days later. Here Howe learned that d'Estaing was somewhere to the south, and sent cruisers to report French movements. On the last day of embarkation they sighted d'Estaing off the Delaware coast, and as he anchored in Delaware Bay on 8 July, Howe sent a warning to Byron. Three days later, Howe learned that d'Estaing was headed north, and that evening the French anchored four miles south of Sandy Hook.

Howe had used the time to perfect his defense. More importantly, he had explained his plan in detail to every subordinate – in contrast to d'Estaing's officers every British captain understood his role. The nearest land north of the channel was beyond cannon range, but to the south a battery of five guns now stood beside Sandy Hook lighthouse. To the west, seven ships were anchored along the south side of the channel, so that each could fire both across it and along it. About three miles east of Sandy Hook, Howe placed a "50" and two frigates to rake d'Estaing's ships as they crossed the bar and then retire. To their north, four galleys would do the same then withdraw to the safety of the Long Island shallows. Another "64" and four frigates formed a reserve[10]. His ships were fully crewed by volunteers from the merchantmen in the harbor, perhaps lured by the prospect of prize money.

These dispositions partially offset d'Estaing's advantage in number and weight of guns, and

Plundering was an inevitable by-product of the years of warfare across New Jersey. During the Monmouth campaign, numerous homes, particularly (but not exclusively) those of Rebel political and military leaders, were plundered during the march, despite the threat of instant execution. However, most accounts point to the women accompanying Clinton's army as the culprits, rather than the troops, and remark on their lawlessness and the failure of anyone to control them. (Private collection)

ensured that every French ship would be raked crossing the bar and passing Sandy Hook[11]. However, once they came alongside the British ships there could be only one outcome; all d'Estaing needed was an easterly wind and a high tide to take him over the bar. Unfortunately, local pilots assured him that the draught (clearance) was only 23ft (7m), a view confirmed by a French officer. In fact it was common for high tides to increase the depth to 30ft (9m) – something Howe had allowed for in planning his defense.

On 22 July, there was a high tide and a northeasterly wind. At 8.00am the French were seen working to windward and by noon there was 30ft of water over the bar. The British expected a fight, but by 3.00pm d'Estaing was heading south and was out of sight by nightfall. The next two days were equally favorable, but there was no sign of the French. On 26 July, Howe sent cruisers to find d'Estaing; they followed him to Delaware Bay, but he eluded them and sailed north to Rhode Island.

In taking three months to cross the Atlantic, and then refusing to chance a battle that he would probably have won (albeit at some cost), d'Estaing lost not one, but two opportunities to end the war. On his arrival in America, Washington wrote: "Had a passage of even ordinary length taken place, Lord Howe with the British ships of war and all the transports in the river Delaware must inevitably have fallen; and Sir Henry Clinton must have had better luck than is commonly dispensed to men of his profession under such circumstances, if he and his troops had not shared at least the fate of Burgoyne."

Without Howe's fleet, Clinton's only route to New York City was overland, with Washington operating on interior lines and outnumbering him. Even had Clinton fought his way through, d'Estaing could still have crossed the bar at his leisure and forestalled any relief by Byron, who could not have kept station for long after an Atlantic crossing. Once Byron withdrew either to Narragansett (where d'Estaing could have blockaded him) or the West Indies, the New York garrison would have no means of supply or escape. This would almost inevitably have led to the demise of a force six times greater than that which surrendered at Saratoga, closely followed by another surrender at Newport.

With no British military base left in North America between Lake Champlain and Florida, lack of manpower and political will would have prevented Lords North and Germain from continuing the war, whatever the objections of the King. The struggle for American independence could have ended in 1778.

View looking south toward Sandy Hook Lighthouse c.1777 by Joseph Des Barres. The main channel into New York City harbor ran east–west (left to right), across the north end of Sandy Hook. Each ship (five "64s", a "50", and a store-ship recently converted from a man-of-war) had its bow to the east (left of picture) and was positioned slightly north of the one ahead to rake any ships entering the harbor with their port broadsides. A spring cable from the port quarter of the six warships allowed them to direct their fire. (National Maritime Museum, London)

Rear Admiral Richard, Viscount Howe (1726–99). "Black Dick" Howe was probably the best naval commander in the Americas and his decision to remain until his replacement arrived may well have prevented a fatal defeat for the British in America. (National Maritime Museum, London)

---

10 Howe's squadron comprised nine ships of the line: *Eagle* (64) flagship, *Trident* (64), *Somerset* (64), *St Albans* (64), *Nonesuch* (64), *Ardent* (64), *Centurion* (50), *Isis* (50), *Experiment* (50); six frigates: *Phoenix* (44), *Roebuck* (44), *Venus* (36), *Pearl* (32), *Richmond* (32), *Apollo* (32); four galleys: *Cornwallis*, *Ferret*, *Hussar*, *Philadelphia*; and one armed storeship: *Leviathan*.
11 D'Estaing's fleet comprised 12 ships of the line: *Languedoc* (90) flagship, *Tonnant* (80), *Cesar* (74), *Zelé* (74), *Guerrier* (74), *Hector* (74), *Marseillais* (74), *Protecteur* (74), *Fantasque* (64), *Provence* (64), *Vaillant* (64), and *Sagittaire* (50); and four frigates: *Aimable* (36), *Alcmêne* (32), *Chimère* (32), and *Engageante* (32).

LEE'S COURT-MARTIAL

Vice Admiral Charles Hector Theobald, Comte d'Estaing (1729–94) by an unknown artist. Originally an army officer, d'Estaing had commanded naval forces during the Seven Years War. He had been captured twice, and imprisoned for violation of parole. Although personally brave, few colleagues credited him with much ability and, like most French admirals, he also suffered from insubordinate political appointees among his captains. (Anne S.K. Brown Collection)

D'Estaing's squadron off the Delaware River trapping the British frigate *Mermaid*. After a three-month voyage from Toulon, d'Estaing arrived off the Delaware on 8 July. The incident with the *Mermaid* (far left) illustrates perfectly how a more timely arrival could have trapped Howe, his fleet, and Clinton's transports. (Library of Congress)

The political fallout from the battle was confined to the Continental Army. On 30 June, Lee, whose name was notably absent from the order congratulating the army, wrote to Washington demanding an explanation for his comments. Instead of an apology, however, Washington sent him notice of a trial for misconduct. That same day Wayne and Scott also wrote to Washington criticizing Lee; their letters arrived after Washington's reply, but he probably knew their views. Lee then sent two more letters to Washington, demanding a court-martial, only to find himself charged with three offences: "disobedience of orders in not attacking the enemy on the 28th of June agreeable to repeated instructions"; "misbehavior before the enemy on the same day, by making an unnecessary, disorderly and shameful retreat"; and "disrespect to the commander in chief in two letters" (written on 29 and 30 June, but wrongly dated 1 July and 28 June).

The court that convened in New Brunswick on 4 July was presided over by Stirling and comprised four brigadier generals (Smallwood, Poor, Woodford, Huntington) and eight colonels, none of whom had been with Lee on the day. Characteristically, Lee chose to defend himself. The first witnesses were Scott and Wayne, both of whom asserted that Washington had wanted a general action, and (wrongly) that Lee had orders to attack "at all events." Mercer, Oswald, and several others supported Lee, and Knox testified that the ground had favored the British. Clinton's force was variously described by Lee's subordinates at anything from 800 to 5,000, the higher figures coming from his supporters, the lower from Washington's. Lee's testimony that he had been facing the British and Hessian Grenadiers, the Foot Guards, the Light Infantry and Hessian Jäger Korps, the Queen's Rangers, both Light Dragoon regiments, and two British line brigades (which would have numbered 10,000 in all) was not far off. Apart from the Jäger Korps and one Light Dragoon regiment, all of those units were present, as was Leslie's 5th Brigade (though that formation saw no fighting).

On 12 August, despite the weight of testimony in his favor, the court convicted Lee of all three charges (but removed "shameful" from the second) and suspended him from Continental service for a year. Either the verdict was a gross miscarriage, or the sentence was astonishingly lenient, and Lee observed that "...[n]o attack it seems can be made on General Washington, but it must recoil on the assailant ..." Although the army and the public at large supported the result, Congress agreed to review the case and it seemed for a while that the decision might be reversed – effectively a vote of "no confidence" in Washington. The charges were considered together rather than separately, and on 5 December, Congress confirmed the verdict, voting six to two by state, and 16 to seven by individuals.

Many senior officers – British and French, as well as American – sympathized with Lee, a view confirmed after the war by Benedict Arnold, who told Clinton that it was only Washington's popularity (and Lee's awful personality) that had led to the verdict being upheld. In Europe, British opinion was that Lee had saved the day, and a French officer remarked that all France believed him innocent.

Both Hamilton and Laurens openly implied in correspondence that Lee's behavior was deliberate and the army had narrowly escaped from a trap. In reality, Lee's conduct during the battle was neither treacherous nor disrespectful to Washington. He obeyed every order prior to 28 June, and his interpretation that those relating to a general engagement were conditional, was not unreasonable. His performance on the day – the lack of any overall plan, contingency orders or reconnaissance – certainly contributed to the retreat, but had more to do with circumstance than his opposition to a major battle (a position shared by several colleagues). In the end, his sound and sensible plan to encircle the British rearguard was thwarted by the terrain, the surprise return of so many British troops, and the behavior of certain subordinates.

Soon after his trial, Lee was wounded in a duel with Laurens over remarks he had made about Washington. Other duels, with Steuben and a member of Congress, were only narrowly avoided. Throughout 1779, Lee alienated many supporters with articles criticizing senior Continental officers, including former friends. As his suspension came to an end, he heard rumors that Congress would dispense with his services and wrote a letter so offensive that, in January 1780, it did just that. Later that year, he went to Philadelphia to sell his estates, and remained there in poverty until his death in October 1782.

D'Estaing's squadron off Sandy Hook. Despite d'Estaing offering a substantial reward, neither the local pilots nor his own officers could find a way across the bar. (Library of Congress)

Lieutenant Colonel Alexander Hamilton (1757–1804) by C.W. Peale. Hamilton had gained fame as an artillery officer, during the New York campaign, before joining Washington's staff as secretary and aide. During the action of 28 June, he had made a rather theatrical proposal to Lee to fight to the death and it was, perhaps fortunate that he was injured and had to go to the rear when his horse was killed under him. (Independence National Historical Park)

CONCLUSION

By any objective criteria, the battle of Monmouth Courthouse was a draw. Clinton thwarted Washington's aim of forcing a major battle, drove back Lee's division in some confusion, and safeguarded his baggage train. For his part, Washington avoided a total disaster (albeit partly of his own making by not supporting Lee more closely) and broke the sequence of defeats that threatened his position as commander in chief. However, whilst two general orders to the army proclaimed victory, his report to

Congress merely mentioned forcing the enemy from the field. Whilst all ranks of his army took great heart from the battle, the unchallenged popular view that they had not only matched the best the enemy had but drove them from the field, is not supported by the facts. Clinton's rearguard had already left the area once and would simply have kept going had Lee not attacked. Between Butler's repulse of the light dragoons at 10.00am and the withdrawal some time after 4.00pm, the British triumphed in every clash (arguably the 42nd were about to fall back anyway when attacked by Cilley), including Wayne's probe at the end of the day: this despite marching almost twice as far as their opponents. The Perrine Ridge position was too strong to assault frontally and once Erskine abandoned his attempt to outflank Washington's left, there was no reason for Clinton to tarry.

For all its noise and duration, the cannonade was at extreme range for the small guns employed and caused relatively little loss. The later counter-attacks were mere tinkering at the edges. Washington took the opportunity to give an already withdrawing foe a low-risk, morale-boosting "push", but Clinton's superiority in cavalry meant he was never seriously threatened. Lee summed up claims of total victory as "a dishonorable gasconade," and while perhaps his view of the battle as a "very handsome check which did the Americans honor" is still debatable, it is closer to the truth.

ORDERS OF BATTLE

THE ROYAL ARMY, 28 JUNE 1778

Commander in chief: Lieutenant-General Sir Henry Clinton

Staff:
Adjutant General: Lieutenant-Colonel Lord Francis Rawdon
Deputy Adjutants General: Major Stephen Kemble, Captain George Hutchinson
Assistant Adjutant General: Lieutenant James Cramond
Quartermaster General: Brigadier-General Sir William Erskine
Commander, Royal Artillery: Brigadier-General James Pattison
Senior Engineer: Captain John Montresor (absent)
Aides-de-camp: Major Duncan Drummond, Captain William Sutherland, Captain Lord
    William Cathcart, Captain William Crosbie, Captain Alexander von Wilmowsky,
    Captain Ernst von Munchhausen
Military Secretary: Captain John Smith
Deputy Inspector General of Provincial Forces: Captain Henry Rooke
Deputy Muster-Master of Provincial Forces: Andrew Bell

Divided between the two divisions:

Artillery – Brigadier-General James Pattison
Royal Artillery	634
Royal Artillery drivers	261
2nd New Jersey Volunteers – LtCol John Morris	129
Hesse Kassel artillery – Maj Heinrich Heitel	39

Non-combatants
Royal Artillery (Civil Branch) – (not known)	51
Engineer's Department – Lt John Hills	138
Bridgemaster's Department – (not known)	21
Black Pioneers – Capt Allen Stewart	49
Wagoners – (not known)	180
Hospital (incl. surgeons) – (not known)	153
Provost and prisoners – (not known)	57
QMG's Department – (not known)	494
Suites, guards and servants – (various)	148
Refugees, women & children – (none)	809

Total: Unattached – 1,063 combatants, 2,100 non-combatants

Second Division – Lieutenant-General Wilhelm von Knyphausen
Flank Guards
17th Light Dragoons – LtCol Samuel Birch	333
2nd Light Infantry – Maj John Maitland	799
40th Foot – LtCol Thomas Musgrave	322

Jäger Korps – Lieutenant-Colonel Ludwig von Wurmb
Hesse-Kassel Jäger (foot) – Maj Ernst von Prueschenk	664
Hesse-Kassel Jäger (mtd.) – Capt August von Wreeden	37
Anspach-Bayreuth Chasseurs – Capt Carl von Cramon	92

1st Brigade – Major-General James Grant
4th Foot – Maj Sir James Murray   321
23rd Foot – LtCol Nesbit Balfour   432
28th Foot – LtCol Robert Prescott   313
49th Foot – LtCol Sir Henry Calder   372

2nd Brigade – Major-General James Grant
5th Foot – Maj George Harris   367
10th Foot – LtCol Francis Smith   135
27th Foot – LtCol Edward Mitchell   340
55th Foot – LtCol Cornelius Cuyler   268

Hessian Brigade – Major-General Johann Stirn
Regiment du Corps (Leib) – Col Friedrich von Wurmb   573
Regiment von Donop – Col David von Gosen   580

Hessian Brigade – Colonel Johann von Loos
Regiment von Alt Lossberg – Col Johann von Loos   276
Regiment von Knyphausen – Maj Johann von Stein   253
Regiment von Woellworth – Col Wolfgang von Woellworth   257

Loyalist Corps
Philadelphia Light Dragoons – Capt Richard Hovenden   116
Bucks County Light Dragoons – Lt Walter Willet   60
Guides and Pioneers – Capt Simon Fraser   206
Roman Catholic Volunteers – LtCol Alfred Clifton   207
Maryland Loyalists – LtCol James Chambers   370
Pennsylvania Loyalists – LtCol William Allen   168
New Jersey Volunteers – LtCol John Van Dike   211
Bucks County Volunteers – Capt William Thomas   76
Recruits – (Various)   53

Total: Second Division – 8,229 all ranks

First Division – Lieutenant-General Charles, Earl Cornwallis

Rearguard

16th Light Dragoons – Maj Francis Gwynne	365
1st Light Infantry – LtCol Robert Abercromby	730
Queen's Rangers – Major John Graves Simcoe	454

British Grenadiers

1st Grenadiers – LtCol William Meadows	761
2nd Grenadiers – LtCol Henry Monckton	737

Hessian Grenadiers – Colonel Heinrich von Kospoth

Battalion Linsing – LtCol Otto von Linsing	411
Battallion Lengerke – LtCol Georg Lengerke	453
Battalion Minnigerode – LtCol Friedrich von Minnigerode	427

Foot Guards – Brigadier-General Edward Mathew

1st Battalion – Col Henry Trelawney	502
2nd Battalion – LtCol James Ogilvie	480

3rd Brigade – Major-General Sir Charles Grey

15th Foot – LtCol Joseph Stopford	352
17th Foot – LtCol Charles Mawhood	330
42nd Foot (2 battalions) – LtCol Thomas Stirling	639
44th Foot – LtCol Henry Hope	334

4th Brigade – (not known; probably also under Major-General Sir Charles Grey)

33rd Foot – LtCol James Webster	365
37th Foot – *(not known)*	386
46th Foot – LtCol Enoch Markham	319
64th Foot – Maj Robert McElroth	426

5th Brigade – Major General Alexander Leslie

7th Foot – LtCol Alured Clarke	333
26th Foot – LtCol Charles Stuart	314
63rd Foot – LtCol James Paterson	305

Total: First Division – 9,440 all ranks

Grand Total: (combat strength only)   **18,732**

NOTES:

1 The two combat divisions are listed in order of march – Knyphausen and then Cornwallis. Strengths are taken from a victualling return made on the morning of 28 June and represents all ranks (i.e. officers and enlisted men).

2. The regiments Alt Lossberg and Knyphausen were designated "fusiliers" but this had no tactical or organizational significance.

3 The Regiment Woellworth was a holding unit for german troops captured at Trenton in 1776, who had escaped subsequently.

4. Probable composition of the British light infantry battalions:

1st Light Infantry – companies from the 4th, 5th, 10th, 15th, 17th, 22nd, 23rd, 27th, 28th, 33rd, 35th, 38th, 42nd, 54th Foot

2nd Light Infantry – companies from the 37th, 40th, 43rd, 44th, 45th, 46th, 49th, 52nd, 55th, 57th, 63rd, 64th, 1/71st, 2/71st Foot

5. Probable composition of the British grenadier battalions:

1st Grenadiers – companies from the 4th, 5th, 10th, 15th, 17th, 22nd, 23rd, 27th, 28th, 33rd, 35th, 38th, 42nd, 55th Foot

2nd Grenadiers – companies from the 38th, 40th, 43rd, 44th, 45th, 46th, 49th, 52nd, 54th, 57th, 63rd, 64th, 1/71st, 2/71st Foot

6. Probable composition of the Hesse-Kassel grenadier battalions:

Linsing – companies from the 2nd and 3rd Foot Guards and Regiments du Corps, Mirbach

Lengerke – companies from the Regiments Prince Carl, Donop, Trumbach, Landgrave

Minnigerode – companies from the Regiments Ditfurth, Prince Hereditaire, Lossberg, Knyphausen

CONTINENTAL ARMY – 28 JUNE 1778

ADVANCE CORPS – OFFICER COMMANDING: MAJOR GENERAL CHARLES LEE

Staff:
Acting Adjutant General: Lieutenant Colonel John Brooks
Aides-de-camp: Captain John Mercer, Captain Evan Edwards
Senior Artillery Officer: Lieutenant Colonel Eleazar Oswald
Deputy Inspector: Jean Baptiste, Chevalier de Ternant
Advisers: Brigadier General David Forman, Colonel the Marquis Francis de Malmedy

Colonel William Grayson's Detachment – **estimated 600 all ranks**
3rd Artillery (2 guns) – Capt Thomas Wells
Grayson's Additional – Col William Grayson
Patton's Additional (part) – LtCol John Parke
4th / 8th /12th Virginia (converged) – Col James Woods

33 officers, 124 NCOs, 15 staff, 455 rank-and-file present and fit for duty
65/237 sick present/absent, 124 on command, and 12 on furlough
16 died, 6 deserted, 5 discharged, and 16 joined/enlisted during June

Colonel John Durkee's Detachment – **estimated 300 all ranks**
3rd Artillery (2 guns) – Capt David Cook
4th / 8th Connecticut (converged) – Col John Durkee
1st / 2nd Rhode Island (converged) – LtCol Jeremiah Olney

52 officers, 118 NCOs, 6 staff, 620 rank-and-file present and fit for duty
73/178 sick present/absent, 98 on command, and 21 on furlough

Brigadier General Anthony Wayne's Command – **estimated 1,000 all ranks**
3rd Artillery (2 guns) – Capt Thomas Seward
Col James Wesson (Learned)[A]
Col Henry Beekman Livingston (Poor)[A]
Col William Stewart (Unattached)[A]

Brigadier General Charles Scott's Command – **estimated 1,440 all ranks**
3rd Artillery (4 guns)
Col Joseph Cilley (Poor)[B]
Col Mordecai Gist (Smallwood)[B]
Col Richard Butler (9th Pennsylvania)[B]
Col Richard Parker (Muhlenberg)[B]

Brigadier General William Maxwell – **estimated 1,000 all ranks (inc. 40–50 cavalry)**
2nd Artillery (2 guns) – Cpt Thomas Randall
Militia Light Horse – LtCol Anthony White
1st New Jersey – Col Matthias Ogden
2nd New Jersey – Col Israel Shreve
3rd New Jersey – Col Elias Dayton
4th New Jersey – Col Ephraim Martin

62 officers, 123 NCOs, 16 staff, 1,096 rank-and-file present and fit for duty
102/186 sick present/absent, 88 on command, and 18 on furlough
13 died, 18 deserted, 1 discharged, and 228 joined/enlisted during June

Colonel Henry Jackson's Detachment – **estimated 200-300 all ranks**
Jackson's Additional – Col Henry Jackson
Lee's Additional – LtCol William Smith
Henley's Additional – Maj John Tyler

OTHER DETACHED CORPS

Colonel Daniel Morgan's Detachment – **estimated 800 all ranks**

Rifle-armed companies   6th, 7th, 8th, 11th Virginia; 1st, 4th, 12th Pennsylvania
Light infantry companies   1st & 2nd North Carolina

"Picked men" *1 officer, 25 other ranks from each of the 13 infantry brigades*
Washington's Guard *2 officers, 80 other ranks*

Attached Militia
1st Monmouth – Col Ahser Holmes
2nd Monmouth – Col Samuel Forman
2nd Burlington – Col Joseph Haight

Approximately 600 Continentals and 217 all ranks

New Jersey Militia – Brigadier General Philemon Dickinson – **estimated 800 all ranks**
Hunterdon Light Horse ^C *serving as Dickinson's guard*
Hunterdon Artillery ^C *serving as infantry*
1st Hunterdon^C – Col Philips
2nd Hunterdon^C – Col Beavers
3rd Hunterdon^C – Col Chambers
4th Hunterdon^C – Col J Taylor
1st Middlesex^C – Col H Van Dike
1st Middlesex^C – Col J Webster
2nd Middlesex^C – Col Neilson
3rd Middlesex^C – Col J Hyer
3rd Monmouth^C – Col D Hendrickson
1st Burlington^C – Col W Shreve
1st Somerset^C – Col F Frelinghuysen
2nd Somerset^C – Col Van Dyke

MAIN BODY – COMMANDER IN CHIEF: GENERAL GEORGE WASHINGTON

Staff:
Adjutant General: Colonel Alexander Scammell
Quartermaster General: Major General Nathanael Greene
Inspector General: Major General Friedrick Wilhelm Augustus von Steuben
Senior Artillery Officer: Brigadier General Henry Knox
Senior Engineer Officer: Brigadier General Louis Lebeque du Portail
Commissary Generals: Colonel Jeremiah Wadsworth, Colonel Clement Biddle
Judge Advocate General: Colonel John Lawrence
Aides-de-Camp: Lieutenant Colonel Alexander Hamilton, Lieutenant Colonel Richard
     Meade, Lieutenant Colonel John Laurens, Lieutenant Colonel John Fitzgerald
Volunteer aides-de-camp: Brigadier General Joseph Reed, Brigadier General John
     Cadwalader
Military Secretary: Lieutenant Colonel Robert Harrison
Assistant Secretary: James McHenry

Right Wing – Major General Nathanael Greene

Brigadier General William Woodford – *44 officers, 46 sergeants, 385 rank-and-file*
3rd/7th Virginia – Col William Heth
11th/15th Virginia – LtCol John Cropper

51 officers, 92 NCOs, 17 staff, 485 rank-and-file fit for duty
18/324 sick present/absent, 183 on command, and 13 on furlough
24 died, 14 deserted, 6 discharged, and 36 joined/enlisted during June

Colonel Thomas Clark (vice BrigGen Lachlan McIntosh) – *28 officers, 28 sergeants,*
    369 rank-and-file
1st North Carolina – Col Thomas Clark
2nd North Carolina – Col John Patten

36 officers, 60 NCOs, 9 staff, 514 rank-and-file present and fit for duty
25/438 sick present/absent, 228 on command, and 7 on furlough
22 died, 13 deserted, 2 discharged, and 114 joined/enlisted during June

Brigadier General Enoch Poor – *58 officers, 57 sergeants, 639 rank-and-file*
1st New Hampshire – **Col Joseph Cilley**
2nd New Hampshire – Col Nathan Hale
3rd New Hampshire – Col Alexander Scammell
2nd New York – Col Philip van Cortlandt
4th New York – **Col Henry Beekman Livingston**

65 officers, 116 NCOs, 10 staff, 788 rank-and-file present and fit for duty
48/723 sick present/absent, 156 on command, and 35 on furlough
27 died, 2 deserted, 12 discharged, and 304 joined/enlisted during June

Brigadier General Jedediah Huntington – *43 officers, 80 sergeants, 639 rank-and-file*
2nd / 5th Connecticut – Col Philip Bradley
1st / 7th Connecticut – Col Heman Swift

60 officers, 148 NCOs, 17 staff, 811 rank-and-file present and fit for duty
96/215 sick present/absent, 174 on command, and 28 on furlough
13 died, 11 deserted, 13 discharged, and 18 joined/enlisted during June

1st Maryland Brigade – *BrigGen William Smallwood* – *61 officers, 72 sergeants, 657 rank-and-file*
1st Maryland – Col John Hawkins Stone
3rd Maryland – Col Mordecai Gist
5th Maryland – Col William Richardson
7th Maryland – Col John Gunby
Delaware – Col David Hall

68 officers, 136 NCOs, 19 staff, 934 rank-and-file present and fit for duty
41/447 sick present/absent, 251 on command, and 27 on furlough
38 died, 25 deserted, and 278 joined/enlisted during June

2nd Maryland Brigade – *BrigGen William Smallwood* – *32 officers, 41 sergeants, 529 rank-and-file*
2nd Maryland – LtCol Thomas Woolford
4th Maryland – Col Josias Carvil Hall
6th Maryland – Col Otho Holland Williams

41 officers, 83 NCOs, 11 staff, 785 rank-and-file present and fit for duty
17/180 sick present/absent, 168 on command, and 16 on furlough
No figures available for losses/additions during June

Brigadier General Peter Muhlenberg – *66 officers, 80 sergeants, 575 rank-and-file*
1st / 5th/ 9th Virginia – **Col Richard Parker**
1st Virginia State – Col George Gibson
2nd Virginia State – Col Gregory Smith
German Battalion – LtCol Ludowick Weltner

70 officers, 150 NCOs, 17 staff, 789 rank-and-file present and fit for duty
65/359 sick present/absent, 165 on command, and 25 on furlough
No figures available for losses/additions during June

Col Christian Febiger? (vice BrigGen George Weedon) – *79 officers, 59 sergeants, 449 rank-and-file*
2nd Virginia – Col Christian Febiger
6th Virginia – Col John Gibson
10th Virginia – Col John Green
14th Virginia – Col William Davies

62 officers, 99 NCOs, 13 staff, 470 rank-and-file present and fit for duty
62/291 sick present/absent, 143 on command, and 37 on furlough
18 died, 6 deserted, 6 discharged, and 38 joined/enlisted during June

Left Wing – Major General William Alexander (Lord Stirling)

1st Pennsylvania Brigade – Col William Irvine (Acting) – *31 officers, 46 sergeants, 352 rank-and-file*
1st Pennsylvania – Col James Chambers
2nd Pennsylvania – Col Henry Bicker
7th Pennsylvania – Col William Irvine
10th Pennsylvania – Col George Nagel

47 officers, 112 NCOs, 9 staff, 514 rank-and-file present and fit for duty
42/74 sick present/absent, 115 on command, and 20 on furlough
No figures are available for losses/additions during June

2nd Pennsylvania Bde. – Col Francis Johnston (Acting) – 35 officers, 51 sergeants,
401 rank-and-file
4th Pennsylvania – **LtCol William Butler**
5th Pennsylvania – Col Francis Johnston
11th Pennsylvania – Col Richard Humpton
1st New York – Col Goose Van Schaick

53 officers, 115 NCOs, 13 staff, 647 rank-and-file present and fit for duty
37/167 sick present/absent, 98 on command, and 13 on furlough
No figures available for losses/additions during June

3rd Pennsylvania Brigade – Col Robert Magaw (Acting) – 39 officers, 56 sergeants,
343 rank-and-file
3rd Pennsylvania – Col Thomas Craig
6th Pennsylvania – LtCol Josiah Harmar
9th Pennsylvania – **Col Richard Butler**
12th Pennsylvania – *formerly* Col William Cooke
Malcolm's Additional – LtCol Aaron Burr
Spencer's Additional – Col Oliver Spencer

42 officers, 112 NCOs, 20 staff, 445 rank-and-file present and fit for duty
53/279 sick present/absent, 171 on command, and 30 on furlough
No figures available for losses/additions during June

Brigadier General John Glover – 63 officers, 61 sergeants, 512 rank-and-file
1st Massachusetts – Col Joseph Vose
4th Massachusetts – Col William Shepard
13th Massachusetts – Col Edward Wigglesworth
15th Massachusetts – Col Timothy Bigelow

85 officers, 129 NCOs, 11 staff, 703 rank-and-file present and fit for duty
44/272 sick present/absent, 187 on command, and 45 on furlough
21 died, 8 deserted, 8 discharged, and 38 joined/enlisted during June

Brigadier General Ebenezer Learned (Absent sick) – 37 officers, 42 sergeants, 294 rank-and-file
2nd Massachusetts – Col John Bailey
8th Massachusetts – Col Michael Jackson
9th Massachusetts – **Col James Wesson**

46 officers, 88 NCOs, 8 staff, 503 rank-and-file present and fit for duty
37/229 sick present/absent, 118 on command, and 47 on furlough
17 died, 4 deserted, 2 discharged, and 23 joined/enlisted during June

Brigadier General John Paterson – 59 officers, 69 sergeants, 357 rank-and-file
10th Massachusetts – Col Thomas Marshall
11th Massachusetts – Col Benjamin Tupper
12th Massachusetts – Col Samuel Brewer
14th Massachusetts – Col Gamaliel Bradford

72 officers, 126 NCOs, 16 staff, 549 rank-and-file present and fit for duty
48 / 312 sick present / absent, 133 on command, and 53 on furlough
24 died, 8 deserted, 6 discharged, and 59 joined/enlisted during June

Unattached
Pennsylvania Det – Capt Anthony Selin (Independent Company)

Artillery – Brigadier General Henry Knox
1st Regiment – Col Charles Harrison
2nd Regiment – Col John Lamb (5 companies)
3rd Regiment – Col John Crane (9 companies)
4th regiment – Capt Francis Proctor (company)
Independent units: Maryland (3 companies)

97 officers, 321 NCOs, 10 staff, 409 rank-and-file present and fit for duty
31 / 68 sick present/absent, 15 on command, and 3 on furlough
9 died, 4 deserted, 5 discharged, and 27 joined/enlisted during June

NOTES:

For Lee's brigades the figure in bold type is the estimated strength present and fit for duty on 28 June; the detailed strengths for permanent formations are from the May 1778 returns, with adjustments based on the subsequent return made at the beginning of July.

For Washington's brigades the figure in bold type is the strength given in an official muster at Manalpan Bridge on 28 June; the detailed strengths listed underneath are from the May 1778 returns, with adjustments based on the subsequent return made at the beginning of July.

Regimental commanders **marked thus** were on detached service with Lee's division and not present with their unit on 28 June.

[A] Detachments are listed by commander in order of State precedence; the original brigade is given in parentheses. Each detachment was probably drawn from several regiments and averaged 350 all ranks.

[B] Detachments are listed by commander in order of State precedence; the original brigade is given in parentheses. Each detachment was probably drawn from several regiments and averaged 360 all ranks.

[C] These units are known to have been on or near the battlefield on 28 June.

THE BATTLEFIELDS TODAY

Although the actual fighting in the Monmouth campaign took place in New Jersey, any tour of the battlefields should begin with the historic areas around Philadelphia. Much of this can be done by public transport or on foot, but a car is needed to follow the routes taken by Clinton and Washington. Allowing for restricted opening times at some locations, all relevant sites could be covered in four or five days.

Valley Forge

It is essential to visit Valley Forge National Historical Park (www.nps.gov.vafo) as this was the moral, as well as geographical, start point of the Monmouth campaign. The park is 18 miles (29km) northwest of Philadelphia, with access from the east and west via Pennsylvania State 23, or the south from Interstates 76 (Schuykill Expressway) and 276 (Pennsylvania Turnpike). The Visitor Center on the east side of the park shows a 20-minute orientation film; from there take either the self-guided car tour or the bus tour (May–September only), which has a taped narrative. Allow a day to appreciate the size of the encampment and to examine the defenses, statues, and Washington's headquarters (the Potts House).

Across the river is the "Schuykill River Trail", which starts just west of Valley Forge and continues into Philadelphia. For those who like walking or cycling, the eastern half of the trail gives some idea of the distance marched by the British to and from Barren Hill. Cross to Betzwood Picnic Area and head east for just over four miles to the site of Swede's Ford, on Swede Street in Norristown. Four miles farther on is Matson's Ford Road in downtown Conshohoken; a mile from the river crossing is a park on Barren Hill Road marking the site of Spring Mill. To the north is Ridge Avenue (the old Ridge Road) and beyond that the northwest section of Fairmile Park, which overlooks parts of the routes taken by Grant and Grey. St Peter's Church still stands atop Barren Hill.

Two roads to Monmouth

It is possible to follow most of the routes taken by the two armies between 18 and 28 June. Starting from Valley Forge, Washington's line of march is easier (as it avoids Philadelphia). Take US Route 202 through Norristown and Doylestown. Avoiding the toll bridge, cross the Delaware on the minor road south of New Hope, into Lambertsville. From there, take County Route 518 east through Hopewell into Rocky Hill. About a mile beyond Rocky Hill the road joins New Jersey State 27. Turn south toward Kingston and from there take County Route 522 east through Dayton and Jamesburg, and then southeast to Englishtown. There you will find the inn (now restored) that was Lee's headquarters on 27 June, and where he and Washington spent the night of 28 June.

OPPOSITE **Like many of the Thirteen Colonies, political divisions within New Jersey were largely dictated by religious differences. St Peter's Church, now in modern-day Freehold, is the last surviving building that stood in the immediate vicinity of Monmouth Courthouse in June 1778 and is typical of the Presbyterian "meetinghouses" found in this part of New Jersey. The church was used as a hospital by the British and 44 badly wounded officers and men were left there after the battle. (Author's photograph)**

The road from Englishtown to Freehold is the same one taken by Lee. Continue southeast on County Route 522 through Tennent, and at the crossroads turn left (i.e. north) to the Meetinghouse. The church still shows signs of its use as a hospital and Monckton's grave is in the cemetery. Returning to the crossroads, head southeast again for just over two miles into Freehold. The Courthouse is no longer there but St Peter's Church is (with its 19th-century steeple), and in Court Street is the battle monument erected in 1884.

Examples of New Jersey farmhouses. New Jersey was an agricultural society and its architecture reflected this. These three views are of preserved or reconstructed farmhouses now standing on the battlefield – clockwise from top left, the Craig Farm, the Wikoff (West Rhea) Farm, and the Sutfin Farm. (Author's photographs)

Clinton's route is rather longer and more interesting. The area around Cooper's Ferry is now built up, but a good starting point is the "Indian King" Tavern on King's Highway East, in Haddonfield. From there head northeast on New Jersey Route 41 to the junction with County Route 537 and turn right (i.e. east) toward Mount Holly. From Mount Holly head north towards Bordentown, which has a number of colonial buildings (including one linked to Napoleon). Then go east to Crosswicks, where the Meetinghouse still has a British cannonball stuck in the upper half of the front wall. It is possible to view the inside of the building and several artifacts, including a map of the engagement on 24 June. Leaving Crosswicks, head north to Allentown via County Route 524. Beyond Allentown take County Route 526 east, passing just north of Imlaystown, until the junction with County Route 537, which heads north into Freehold. As you enter Freehold, the Covenhoven House still stands on West Main Street and is open from May to September.

Beyond Freehold, the road system has changed somewhat, and it is not possible to follow Clinton's and Knyphausen's routes exactly. However, Holmdel (en route to Middletown) contains a typical 1750s Dutch farmhouse, and the Allen House in Shrewsbury (restored to its 1778 status as a tavern) has an exhibit on the battle. The original Sandy Hook lighthouse is still there, and operational, and can be toured (http://www.nps.gov/gate/pphtm/facilities.html).

Monmouth Battlefield

Monmouth Battlefield State Park, run by the New Jersey State Park Service (www.njparksandforests.org), is 12 miles (19km) east of the New

Jersey Turnpike (exit 8) on New Jersey Route 33, or 15 miles (24km) south of the Garden State Parkway (exit 123) via US Route 9 and New Jersey Business Route 33. The 2,000-acre site covers the area of the afternoon action, and extensive efforts have been made to restore the land to how it appeared on 28 June, with orchards, crop fields and woodland. One of the farms – the Craig House – has been restored and a substantial visitor center on Comb's Hill provides a panoramic view of the Parsonage Farm and the Hedgerow, across to Perrine Ridge and the Sutfin Farm. To cover the battlefield properly requires a full day and, in addition to the historical facilities, there are 25 miles (40km) of walking, riding and cycling trails.

Another local site of interest is the Monmouth County Historical Association, based at 70 Court Street, in Freehold. The Association operates several historic sites – including the period buildings in Holmdel, Middletown and Shrewsbury – as well as a library, and a museum with military relics of the battle.

FURTHER READING

The confused nature of the battle is reflected in the writings of both participants and historians, and may explain why so few books have been published on the subject. W. Stryker's *The Battle of Monmouth* (New York, 1927) is still good, but new research and interpretation, particularly by Dr Garry Stone of Monmouth Battlefield Park, has exposed errors (possibly due to the premature death of the author and the book's completion by a non-military editor). Samuel S. Smith's *The Battle of Monmouth* (Monmouth Beach, NJ, 1964) uses first-hand accounts recorded within a few years of the battle, but was written when many fewer documents were available, and poor editing left strange "gaps" in the action and unexplained alternative names for parts of the battlefield. In addition, the author did not understand the ad hoc nature of Lee's detachments and assumed that all officers were serving with their own regiment. T. Thayer's *Washington and Lee at Monmouth – the making of a scapegoat* (London, 1976) focuses on the rivalry between the two men and the court-martial, clearly supporting Lee.

Several well-known diaries contain first-hand accounts of the battle, including J.P. Martin's *Private Yankee Doodle* (New York, 1962), J. Greenman's *Diary of a Common Soldier in the American Revolution* (DeKalb, Ill, 1978), and H. Dearborn's *Revolutionary War Journals of Henry Dearborn, 1775–1783* (Chicago, Ill, 1939). Other useful sources include private letters, pension applications, and the witness depositions from Lee's court-martial. British accounts include: J. Peebles, *John Peebles' American War 1776–1782* (Stroud, 1998); J. Simcoe, *A history of the operations of a partisan corps called the Queen's Rangers* (New York, 1968); and B. Uhlendorf, *Revolution in America: The Baurmeister Journals* (New Brunswick, NJ, 1957).

For information on the commanders it is worth consulting D.S. Freeman's *George Washington: A Biography, Vol 5: Victory with the help of France* (New York, 1952), J.R. Alden's *General Charles Lee: Patriot or Traitor* (Baton Rouge, 1951), B. Willcox's *Portrait of a general: Sir Henry Clinton in the War of Independence* (New York, 1964), and *The American Rebellion: The British Commander-in-Chief's Narrative of his campaigns 1775–1782* (New Haven, 1954) by the same author. Strangely, F. & M. Wickwire's *Cornwallis and the War of Independence* (London, 1971) has little on the battle, and there seems to be no biography of Knyphausen outside the unreliable *Appleton's Cyclopedia of American Biography* (New York, 1888).

R. Hinde's *Discipline of the Light Horse* (London, 1778) and J. Fuller's *British Light Infantry in the 18th Century* (London, 1925) provide useful insights into British tactics, and the Public Records Office at Kew has detailed returns for Clinton's army. However, there is nothing comparable for Washington's army (especially Lee's force) beyond the brigade strengths quoted in Stryker, though there are detailed monthly returns in C.H. Lesser's *The Sinews of Independence* (Chicago, 1976). R. Wright's *The Continental Army* (Washington, DC, 1989) explains the structure of the Continental Army in 1778.

For naval operations (often overlooked) see Sir W. Clowes' (ed.) *The Royal Navy: A History from the earliest times to 1900, Volume 3* (London, 1893). Some contemporary maps are included in W. Marshall's and H. Peckham's *Campaigns of the American Revolution* (New Jersey, 1976), and D. Higginbotham's and K. Nebenzahl's *Atlas of the American Revolution* (New York, 1974). General works, placing the Monmouth campaign in context, are listed in the bibliographies of Campaign 37 **Boston 1775** and Campaign 47 **Yorktown 1781**.

INDEX

Figures in **bold** refer to illustrations

Alexander, MajGen William (aka Lord Stirling) **38**
  and Lee's court-martial 79
  and march from Valley Forge 29, 39, 40
  at Monmouth 50–1, 58–9, 70
American militias **22**
  in action 36–7, **36**, 47
  New Jersey 25, 30, 58–9, 76
  organization 25
  Pennsylvania 30
  Somerset 50–1, 58–9
American troops *see* American militias;
  Continental Army
Anspach-Bayreuth troops 21, 33
  see also Hessian troops
Arnold, Benedict 7, 40, 80
artillery 20, 25, **66–8**

baggage trains **11**
Barren Hill, action at (1778) 30–2, **31**
Bell, Andrew 76
Bennington, battle of (1777) 8
Board of War, role and membership 27–8
Bordentown 30, 37, 92
Brandywine, battle of (1777) 8
British and ally troops
  at Barren Hill (1778) 30–2, **31**
  commanders 15–17
  march across New Jersey 33–7, **35**, **36**, 40–4
  at Monmouth 44–74
  organization and formations 19–23
  winter in Philadelphia (1777) 29
  withdrawal 58–9, 73–7
  see also British Regulars; Hessian troops;
    Loyalist troops
British Regulars
  organization 19–20
British Regulars: brigades
  1st 35, 47, 75
  2nd 35, 47, 75
  3rd 35, 42–3, 47, 48, 50–1, 58–9, 64, 65, 71, 75
  4th 35, 42–3, 47, 50–1, 58–9, 75
  5th 35, 42–3, 47, 50–1, 58–9, 75
British Regulars: Foot Guards 19, 47, 50–1, **54–6**, 58–9, 69, 73, 75
  7th 42–3, 50–1, 58–9
  10th 35, 47
  15th 42–3, 50–1, 58–9
  17th 30, 42–3, 47, 50–1, 58–9
  26th 42–3, 50–1, 58–9
  27th 30
  28th 35
  33rd 42–3, 50–1, 58–9, **66–8**, 74
  37th 42–3, 50–1, 58–9
  40th 47
  42nd 42–3, 50–1, 58–9, **62–4**, 70, 71, 73
  44th 42–3, 50–1, 58–9, 71
  46th 30, 42–3, 50–1, 58–9
  49th 47
  55th 35

  63rd 42–3, 50–1, 58–9
  64th 42–3, 50–1, 58–9
British Regulars: Grenadiers 47
  1st 42–3, 47, 49, 50–1, 58–9, **66–8**, 69–70, 73–4, **89**
  2nd 42–3, 47, 50–1, 58–9, 69–70
British Regulars: light dragoons **20**, 75
  16th 20, 35, 42–3, 47, 50–1, **54–6**, 58–9, 69
  17th 20, 35
British Regulars: light infantry **20**
  1st 30, 35, 36, 42–3, 47, 49, 50–1, 58–9, 64, 71
  2nd 30, 47
Brooks, LtCol John 52, 53, 61, 70
Bunner, LtCol Rudolph 74
Burgoyne, John 8–9
Burr, Aaron **40**, 74
Butler, Col Richard 42–3, 46, 48–9, 50–1, 52, 53, 70
Byron, Vice Adm the Honourable John 77

Cadwalader, BrigGen John 40
Canada, war in 7, 8
Carleton, Gov. Guy 7, 8
Carlisle, Earl of 27, 33
Carlisle Peace Commission 27, 33
casualties 76
Chappell, Alonzo, paintings by **89**
Charleston, attack on (1776) 8, 15, 17
Cilley, Col Joseph 50–1, 52, 58–9, 60, **62–4**, 70–1, 73
Clinton, LtGen Sir Henry **8**, 15–16
  appointment as C in C 30
  at Barren Hill (1778) 31–2
  and Carlisle Peace Commission 33
  and Cornwallis 17
  march across New Jersey 32, 33–7
  at Monmouth 42–3, 46, 47–8, 69, 71
  on his officers 19
  withdrawal 58–9, 73–7
Comb's Hill **66–8**, **69**, 73, 74
Continental Army
  artillery 25, **66–8**
  at Barren Hill (1778) 30–2, **31**
  cavalry 24
  and Clinton's march, harassment of **35**, 36–7, **36**, 40–4
  commanders 17–18
  infantry 24
  march from Valley Forge 39–44
  march to New York City 76–7
  at Monmouth 44–74
  organization and formations **22**, 23–5, **23**, 39, 40
  Steuben's training 28, 29, **30**
  in Valley Forge (1777–78) 27, 28–9, **30**
Continental Army: brigades
  Conway's 39, 40, 70–3, 73–4
  Du Plessis' 50–1
  Durkee's 42–3
  Glover's 39, 40, 50–1, 58–9, 70–3
  Huntington's 39, 40, 50–1, 58–9, 70–3
  La Fayette's 42–3

  Learned's 39, 40, 50–1, 58–9, 70–3
  Maryland 39, 40, 58–9, 71, 74
  Maxwell's 40, 42–3, 46, 52, 53, 57, 58–9, 61, 65, 76, 77
  Morgan's 24, **36**, 39–40, 76
  Muhlenberg's 39, 40, 74
  North Carolina 39, 40, 58–9, 71, 74
  Patterson's 39, 40, 74
  Pennsylvania 39, 40, 50–1, 58–9, 70–3
  Poor's 30, 32, 39, 40, 58–9, 71, 74
  Proctor's 50–1, 58–9
  Scott's 39, 40, 41, 42–3, 46, 50–1, 52, 53, 58–9, **62–4**, 70, 71
  Varnum's 39, 40, 41, 42–3, 46
  Virginia 58–9
  Wayne's 42–3, **66–8**, **89**
  Weedon's 39, 40, 71
  Woodford's 39, 40, 50–1, 73, 74
Continental Army: regiments
  1st Pennsylvania 76
  3rd Pennsylvania 58–9, 73–4
  Malcolm's Additional 58–9, 73–4
  New Jersey 42–3, 50–1, 52, 53, 58–9, 61, 65, 71
  Spencer's Additional 58–9, 73–4
Conway, Thomas 27
Conway Cabal 27–8, 39
Cooper's Ferry 33
Cornwallis, LtGen Charles, Earl **15**, 16–17
  and march across New Jersey 35, 36, 37
  Monmouth and after 42–3, 47, 48, 49–52, 75
Coryell Ferry 40
Covenhoven House **44**, 92
Craig Farm 48, 50–1, 53, 70, **92**, 93
Crane, John 25
Crosswicks 36–7, **36**, **37**, 92

Dearborn, LtCol Henry **62–4**
deserters 35, 76
Dickinson, BrigGen Philamon 29, 40, 41, 44–6, 71
Du Plessis, Thomas-Antoine de Mauduit 52–3, 58–9, **66–8**, 73
Du Portail, BrigGen Louis Lebeque de Presle 29, 37, 42–3, **47**, 57
Duplessis, Joseph, portraits by **26**
Durkee, Col John 46, 47, 49

East Rhea Farm 57
Eden, Sir William 27, 33
Edwards, Capt Evan 44, 52, 53, 70
Erskine, BrigGen Sir William **11**, 37, 58–9, 64, 71–3, 74
Estaing, Vice Adm Charles Hector Theobald, Comte d' 77–8, **79**

Fitzgerald, LtCol John 41–2, 60–1
Forman, Gen David 44
formations 20–1, **22**, **23**
Foster, BrigGen James 30
France, joins war 26–7, 29
Franklin, William 12

Gainsborough, Thomas, portraits by **31**

Gates, MajGen Horatio 27
Germain, Lord George 8, 15, 26
German troops *see* Hessian troops
Germantown, battle of (1777) 8
Gist, Col Mordecai 42, 50–1, 70, 85, 87
Grant, Capt **62–4**
Grant, MajGen James 31–2, **32**, 33
Grayson, Col William
  at Monmouth: Lee's advance 41, 42–3, 44, 46
  at Monmouth: Lee's retreat 50–1, 52, 53, 61
Greene, MajGen Nathanael 29, 40, 50–1, 58–9, 68, **72**, 73
Grey, MajGen Sir Charles 31–2, 42–3, 50–1, 58–9, **65**, 74

Hamilton, LtCol Alexander 40, 60, 70, **80**
Harrison, Charles 25
Harrison, LtCol Robert 27, 60–1
Hayes, Mary Ludwig **75**
Hessian troops 20–1, **21**
  at Barren Hill (1778) 31–2
  commander 16, **16**
  deserters and casualties 77
  and march across New Jersey 33, 35
  at Monmouth 42–3, 47, 50–1, 52, 58–9, 75
  Stirn's troops 35, 75
Howe, Rear Adm Lord Richard 8, 15, 30, 77–8, **78**
Howe, LtGen Sir William **31**
  as C in C 8, 15, 20, 21, 29, 31–2
  recall 30, 32

Indian King tavern, Haddonfield **32**

Jackson, Col Henry 41, 42–3, 46, 48–9, 50–1, 52–3, 65
Johnstone, George 27, 33

Ker Farm 57, 61
Knox, BrigGen Henry 25, **61**, 68, 70, **71**, 79
Knyphausen, LtGen Wilhelm Freiherr von 16, **16**
  and march across New Jersey 33, 35, 36, 37
  at Monmouth and after 42–3, 47, 75
Kospoth, Col Heinrich von 42–3, 50–1, 58–9

La Fayette, MajGen the Marquis de **19**
  at Barren Hill (1778) 30–2
  and Canada 27–8
  and march from Valley Forge 29, 37, 39, 40–1
  at Monmouth 42–3, 49, 50–1, 53, 58–9, 61, 71
Lacey, BrigGen John 30
Lamb, John 25
Laurens, LtCol John 70, **76**, 80
Ledyard, Maj Benjamin 53
Lee, MajGen Charles **7**, 17–18, **17**
  before campaign 29, 37, 40
  court-martial 79–80
  duel with Laurens 76, 80
  and march from Valley Forge 39–44
  on Monmouth 81
  at Monmouth: advance on courthouse 42–9
  at Monmouth: replaced and after 56, **57**, 60–5, 69
  at Monmouth: retreat from courthouse 49–53, 57–60
  on New Jersey 9
  relations with Washington 18
Leslie, BrigGen the Honourable Alexander **31**
  and march across New Jersey 33, 35, 36, 37
  at Monmouth 42–3, 50–1, 58–9
Leutze, Emmanuel, paintings by **57**
Livingston, Col Henry 42–3, 49, 50–1, 53, 57, 65

Livingston, Gov. William 12, 15
Louis XVI, king of France 26, **26**
Loutherbourg, P.J. de, drawings by **20**
Loyalist troops 21–3
  Guides and Pioneers 21, 35
  Maryland Loyalists 35
  New Jersey Volunteers 21, 30
  Provincials 35
  Queen's Rangers 21–3, 30, 35, 36, 42–3, 46, 47, 48, 49, 50–1, 58–9, 71–3
  Roman Catholic Volunteers 35

McBarron, paintings by **23**
McHenry, Dr James 49, 65
McLane, Maj Allen 30, 39
Martin, Joseph Plumb 64, 75
Mathew, BrigGen 42–3, 50–1, 58–9
Mawhood, Col Charles 30
Maxwell, BrigGen William
  and Clinton's march across New Jersey 35, 40
  at Monmouth 14, 42–3, 46, 49, 50–1, 52, 53, 58–9, 85
  Monmouth aftermath 76
Mercer, Capt John 48, 52–3, 61, 65, 69, 70, 79
Mermaid **79**
Mifflin, MajGen Thomas 27, 28, 39
Monckton, LtCol Henry 44, 50–1, 70, **76**, 92
Monmouth Courthouse 12, **34**
  battle and battlefield **39**, 42–74, 80–1, 92–3
Montgomery, Richard 7
Montresor, Capt John 33
Morgan, Col Daniel 39–40, **40**, 44, 53–7, 76

naval engagements 77–8, **79**, **80**
New England, map **10**
New Jersey
  Clinton's march across 33–7
  farmhouses **92**
  geography and history 9
  militia 25, 30, 58–9, 76
  politics and people 9–12
  soldiers raised 12
New York City 8, 9, 17, 77

Ogden, Col Matthias 50–1, 53, 60, 61, 65, 69
Olney, LtCol Jeremiah 42–3, 49, 50–1, 53, 57, 65, 70
Oswald, LtCol Eleazar
  and Lee's court-martial 79
  at Monmouth: Lee's advance 42–3, 47, 48
  at Monmouth: Lee's retreat 50–1, 52, 53, 57, 65, 69–70

Parke, LtCol John 42–3, 50–1, 85
Parker, Col Richard 50–1, 58–9, 60, **62–4**, 70–1, 73
Parsonage Farm 50–1, 58–9, 68, 69–70, **71**, **89**
Patterson, BrigGen John 74
Peale, C.W., portraits by **18**, **19**, **29**, **38**, **40**, **47**, **61**, **72**, **76**, **80**
Peale, R., portraits by **52**
Perrine Ridge 48, 50–1, **61**, **69**, 70–3, **70**
Philadelphia **8**
  British occupation and evacuation 8, 11, 16, 29, 33
  American re-entry 39, 40
Pickering, Col Thomas 27
Pitcher, Molly **75**
plundering **77**
Poor, BrigGen Enoch 30
Potter, BrigGen James 30
Proctor, John 25
Pulaski, Casimir 24

Quebec, siege of (1775) 7

Ramsay, LtCol Nathaniel 49, 50–1, **52**, 53, **54–6**, 65–9
Reynolds, Sir Joshua, portraits by **11**
Rhea, LtCol David 68, 73
Rogers, Robert 21

Saint Peter's Church **90**
Sandy Hook 77–8, **78**, **80**
Saratoga, battle of (1777) 9
Scott, BrigGen Charles
  and Clinton's march across New Jersey 40
  and Lee's court-martial 79
  at Monmouth 42–3, 47, 49, 50–1, 52, 53, 58–9, 61
Seward, Capt Thomas 49, 50–1
Simcoe, John Graves 21
Skinner, Cortland 21
slaves 11
Smith, LtCol William 50–1, 52, 65
Spotswood Middle Brook 42–3, 47–8, 52, **53**, **54–6**, 58–9, 60, **60**, 64, 73
Steuben, MajGen "Baron" Friedrich von **29**
  and Clinton's march across New Jersey 40
  and Lee 80
  at Monmouth 50–1, 58–9, 71, 74
  and strategy 37
  training Continental Army 28, 29, **30**
Stewart, Col Walter 42–3, 49, 50–1, 53, **54–6**, 57, 65–9
Stirling, Lord *see* Alexander, MajGen William
Sutfin Farm and orchard 50–1, 58–9, **61**, **62–4**, **69**, **70**, 73, **92**

Tennent Meetinghouse **45**, 46, 50–1, 60
Trelawney, Col Henry 69
Trenton, battle of (1776) 8
Trumbull, Joseph 27

uniforms and clothing **7**, **20**

Valley Forge **27**, 28–9, **28**, **30**, 91
Van Cortlandt, Col Philip 40
Vanderlyn, John, portraits by **40**
Vergennes, Charles Gravier, Comte de 26, **27**

Washington, Gen George **7**, 18, **18**, **75**
  and Conway Cabal 27–8
  on d'Estaing 78
  Lee replaced 56, **57**, 60–5
  and Lee's court-martial 79
  and march from Valley Forge 40–4, 46
  at Monmouth 58–9, 64, 68, 70, 73–4
  Monmouth aftermath 76–7
  New York City, defense of 8
  relations with Lee 18
  strategy 28–9, 37–8, 40
Watson, James, portraits by **65**
Wayne, BrigGen Anthony
  and Lee's court-martial 79
  march from Valley Forge 39–40
  at Monmouth: American delaying action 56, 65–9
  at Monmouth: Clinton's withdrawal 58–9, 73–4
  at Monmouth: Lee's advance and retreat 42–3, 46, 48, 49, 50–1, 52, 53–7, 68
  at Monmouth: Parsonage Farm 68, **89**
Webster, LtCol James 42–3, 50–1, 58–9, 73
Wesson, Col James 42–3, 49
West Rhea Farm *see* Wikoff Farm
White, LtCol Anthony 42–3, 48, 50–1
Wikoff, Capt Peter 60, 61
Wikoff Farm **47**, **49**, 50–1, 58–9, **92**
Woodford, BrigGen William 50, 52–3, 58–9, 86
Woods, Col James 69